AF573731

A City at Risk

A City at Risk

A Contemporary Look at London's Streets

SIMON JENKINS

With illustrations by David Larkham

HUTCHINSON OF LONDON

HUTCHINSON & CO. (*Publishers*) LTD.
178–202 Great Portland Street, London W1

London Melbourne Sydney
Auckland Johannesburg Cape Town
and agencies throughout the world

First published 1970

This book has been set in Baskerville and printed in Great Britain on Evensyde Cartridge by Benham and Company Limited, Colchester, Essex.

ISBN 0 09 104760 9

Acknowledgments

This book arose out of a series entitled 'Looking at London' in the London *Evening Standard*. Without the scope allowed me by its editor, Charles Wintour, it would never have been written. I am also indebted to Anne Riches of the G.L.C. Historic Buildings Division, without whose constant tutelage in matters architectural I should never have found the confidence to make some of my brasher judgments. Needless to say, neither she nor her employers should be held responsible for any of them. I should also like to thank All Souls' College, Oxford, for hospitality and visual inspiration during the writing of the last chapter. And special thanks go to Carol Flynn for typing out the whole work with phenomenal speed and efficiency.

I owe a different kind of debt to those on whose work I inevitably found myself perpetually drawing. More than once during the reading of works such as Sir Nikolaus Pevsner's *Buildings of England*, Sir John Summerson's *Georgian London* and David Piper's *Companion Guide to London*, I asked myself whether I could ever hope to say it better. Any apparent plagiarism on my part is not out of idleness but out of respect.

Contents

Illustrations

Introduction

This book is about the streets of London. It is intended partly as a guide, partly as an essay and partly as a call to arms. Its theme is that there is a uniqueness in London's appearance which successive waves of development have threatened, but usually managed eventually to enhance. And its concern is that the wave that has been under way for the past decade is of such a peculiar order of magnitude that the threat may for once prove too much.

I have placed the emphasis on streets rather than on particular buildings, because, in terms of their impact on the character of London, they are far more important. St. Paul's Cathedral is one of Europe's great architectural monuments—of which London happens to be the proud possessor. The view of St. Paul's up Ludgate Hill, however, is pure London. A street provides, by its scale and its style, the vital context for a fine building. But more than that, a street is architecture at its most all-pervading. The streets of London provide the most public—and the most comprehensive—of the capital's museums of art. As a museum, it is the most often visited, the most often observed and commented upon and it has the most rapidly changing exhibits. It is one which is used by everyone and from which everyone, albeit often subconsciously, drives aesthetic pleasure or displeasure.

And yet, as a comprehensive work of art, London's street architecture is still frequently treated with quite phenomenal neglect. A nation which would rightly be horrified were anyone to discuss the contents of the National Gallery solely in terms of the value of the space they occupy, can still use precisely the same terms to describe the buildings of Whitehall.

This book is an attempt in part to rectify this neglect. The final chapter deals with the background to the conservation of London's physical character. It looks at the problems which have arisen in the past and at the controls that have been evolved to meet them. It examines in particular the loopholes that still exist and the potential damage that could arise from our failure to plug them.

There can be no better source material for such conclusions, however, than the present appearance of the streets themselves. In the course of 1969 I wrote, in the *Evening Standard*, a column entitled 'Looking at London', which described—often highly subjectively—a number of London streets and delved occasionally into their hinterland. This series, extended and substantially rewritten, forms the bulk of this book. Historical background is kept to a minimum, as are lengthy descriptions of individual buildings. And since this is a book about the appearance of streets, there is no mention made (except very rarely in passing) of interiors. Most of these that are open to public view are anyway dealt with in the usual guide-books.

The idea has been quite deliberately to create an impression of streets and squares as a visual unity, emphasising the interaction of different buildings and views with one another. The thirty streets described are not chosen arbitrarily from among the thousands in central London. They are, in my opinion, the most interesting visually, either in themselves or as introductions to a particular area or style of buildings. Fewer than thirty would not have been sufficient, and more would have become repetitive. As they stand, they cover most of the better-known areas of London, representing in so far as this is possible most of the stages of its development. They have been grouped into seven districts, each of which could be encompassed in a fairly brisk afternoon's walk.

Since, however, I have tried first and foremost to describe simply what is visible here and now, rather than go into past history, it is worth looking briefly at the various stages by which the London street has arrived where it is today, and at some of the styles and the architects which have been major influences on its development. For these influences form a recurring theme in the succeeding chapters.

The medieval City of London has now disappeared almost completely. In 1666 the City was burnt out, and the few medieval and Tudor streets that were outside the Fire area have long since succumbed to commercial pressures for redevelopment. Those buildings that have survived to this day contribute virtually nothing to the City's character and remain chiefly as museum pieces dotted about among later developments. A number of stone-built churches survived the Fire or were reconstructed in their original style, and sections of the old Inns of Court still stand—saved by the rock solid conservatism of those institutions. And there are, of course, such great historical monuments of Church and State as Westminster Abbey, St. Stephen's Hall and Inigo Jones's Banqueting Hall.

But the medieval City of London did bequeath one asset of crucial importance to an understanding of the pattern of streets in the modern city centre. And that was its street layout. For a variety of reasons, which we shall examine later, the city that was rebuilt after 1666 was not really a new one at all, although most of the buildings were. Precious little new street planning was done. And the absence since that day of any bold dictator to do to London what Napoleon did to Paris, or Pope Sixtus had done to Rome, has meant that the streets of the City of London and the route along the river to Westminster bear all the marks of a medieval town, even today. Virtually none are straight, and most are very short. Right-angled turns are few and the streets are punctuated by innumerable courts and passages which now look absurd, but which once formed a vital means of access to stables and rows of smaller houses behind the main thoroughfares. The north flank of Fleet Street provides a good example of this, escaping as it did even the modest rationalisation of the post-Fire reconstruction.

This medieval street pattern undeniably had a limiting effect on the scale of later development. The fragmented system of land tenure, in particular, has made comprehensive redevelopment very difficult. This, in turn, has restrained the scale of modern central London and allowed pockets of old buildings to survive alongside the new—conserving an architectural and social variety that is one of London's most distinctive features.

Whatever may be the background to the street plan, however, the London that can be seen today is basically a city just three centuries old. The experience of the Great Fire and the rebuilding that followed it added a tremendous expansion out of the City and Westminster area to the 'suburbs' round about them. The late seventeenth century was the age, not just of Sir Christopher Wren and the new churches and company halls but of the Rebuilding

Acts of 1667 and 1670, and of great developers such as Lord Southampton and Nicholas Barbon. The pressure to expand and the immense demand this created meant that not just houses but whole estates were developed as speculative ventures. The necessity for using brick, the advent of simple and economical building designs and the availability of land resulted in a new city of spacious streets and squares and handsome individual houses. Sadly, little survives even of this period, though there are plenty of individual public buildings still standing. The only comparatively intact seventeenth-century squares and rows are those preserved in the Inns of Court and the streets round them. Houses of this period are still easily recognisable by their red brick and wooden surrounds to their windows. The only ornament was round the doors—in the form of varieties of pillars and pediments usually in wood but occasionally (as in the Inner Temple) in sculpted brick.

With the eighteenth century and the reign of Queen Anne, the English baroque tradition begun by Wren flourished in public works by Vanbrugh, Hawksmoor and Archer. Many of these, particularly churches, survive. Their style, however, proved remarkably short-lived. For the most significant architectural development of the eighteenth century was the growth of the Palladian movement under the patronage of Lord Burlington. Its peculiar brand of academic classicism nipped the growth of English baroque in the bud and dictated the course of British architecture throughout the period when continental countries were advancing through High Baroque and Rococo to their own more grandiose classical revivals. The extraordinary restraint of the style, based on the strict renaissance classicism of the Italian, Palladio, and on the English variety initiated by Inigo Jones in the early seventeenth century, was swiftly reflected in public and private building at every level. Buildings such as the New Buildings in Lincoln's Inn and Somerset House in the Strand, by Sir Robert Taylor and Sir William Chambers respectively, are excellent examples. The characteristic stone façade, with carefully proportioned pillars and pediment built up on a simple rusticated ground floor, was the dominant style of public buildings right through to the days of the Regency.

Meanwhile the London domestic house ceased to be the individually designed mansion that it had been at the time of

Wren—or even the simple but rather slapdash buildings produced by men such as Barbon. It had, in the first place, been given a new uniformity by further Building Acts passed in 1707 and 1709, laying down still more fire-proofing precautions. No wooden facings were to be allowed, which meant that the old wooden eaves had to become stone parapets and window-frames were to be recessed four inches back into the brick of the walls. Under Palladian influence, the town house became increasingly part of a consistent street design. Each terrace or block was viewed as a whole, often with such features as pillars or pilasters in the central section and a pediment on top, as if to create an impression of a single mansion. The simple Palladian ground floor was reflected in the added importance accorded to the first floor, where the major rooms were now situated. And every door and window had to accord, except in the smallest detail, to the character of the whole row. The street was at last more than merely the sum of its individual parts—and it remained so for nearly a century and a half.

The first streets that can be said to have been designed on Palladian principles were those, naturally enough, on the Burlington Estate north of Piccadilly in Mayfair. The first square that anyone attempted to co-ordinate on a Palladian pattern was Grosvenor Square, by the developer Edward Shepherd, who also gave his name to Shepherd Market. Nothing of his work survives in Grosvenor Square. But Bedford Square—the finest square of its type in London—lives on, while the sad relics of the Adam Brothers' Portland Place and Adelphi developments illustrate how vital overall consistency was to the visual success of each individual house. Later in the eighteenth century and into the nineteenth, the exploding and wealthy population of London spread out into areas such as St. Pancras, Marylebone, Bayswater, Belgravia and Pimlico, faithfully carrying with them the architecture and the street design of the early Georgians. And they still did it with a speculative panache that enabled large estates to be planned on an unprecendented scale. This estate system, another distinctive feature of London's development, has preserved most of these neighbourhoods intact to a remarkable degree—though the Portman Estate is still being permitted gaily to knock down areas of Georgian Marylebone. What major redevelopment has taken place has, for the most part, been confined to strips along the main thoroughfares—meaning that a sightseer who sticks to the main roads will get a far from accurate picture of the true character of the western side of London. It is the estates behind them that are frequently architectural monuments, every bit as significant and valuable as the great buildings of London that are so much better known.

The closing years of the Georgian period and the early reign of Queen Victoria saw the restrained classicism which had so dominated the planning and architecture of Georgian London begin to give way. The classicism itself became freer—as can be seen in the tremendous schemes of John Nash for the redevelopment of huge areas of West London under the patronage of the Prince Regent. The continued march of the great estates, chiefly under the phenomenal energy of Thomas Cubitt, gradually took on a less disciplined, more Italianate appearance. Cornices and porches became more ornate and stucco was slapped on new and old buildings alike. And as the Victorian era progressed, the classicism itself started to disappear. The columns and friezes of the United Services and Athenaeum Clubs in Pall Mall gave way to the renaissance *palazzi* of Charles Barry's Travellers and Reform Clubs next door.

The second half of the nineteenth century also saw the first major exercises in the redevelopment of the old heart of London. The old streets, still dating from the time of the Great Fire, suddenly began to sprout Italianate and Gothic offices. Stylistic innovation became the rage, particularly in public buildings. The great architects of the High Victorian era were expected to be able to turn their hand to whatever style might suit their massively wealthy clients. Men such as Sir George Gilbert Scott could design the Foreign Office—in a High Victorian renaissance style—and follow it almost immediately with St. Pancras in an equally High Gothic. Smaller institutions such as banks, clubs and commercial firms all demanded distinctive monuments to their corporate individuality—and preferably wealth—rather than following the Georgian conformity to classical 'good taste'. The central London streets lost their uniform appearance, and suffered at the same time their second increase in physical scale since Tudor times. London, central area and suburbs taken as a whole, was no longer a city bound together visually by the character of Georgian street architecture and classical public buildings. It became heterogeneous, and has remained so to this day.

In the closing years of the century, the conflicting Gothic and Italianate styles were overtaken in their turn by a wave of Dutch Renaissance and 'Queen Anne' revival—chiefly under the impact of architects such as Richard Norman Shaw. Nor was it merely a style, as the others had chiefly been, for public and major commercial buildings. Small offices and shops along main streets such as Oxford Street, Bishopsgate and Brompton Road blossomed with steep gables, mullioned windows and a fantastic assortment of motifs. Georgian Hans Town was rebult in Pont Street 'Dutch'—and was imitated endlessly. Red brick and terracotta were all the rage and nothing was worse than simplicity. Some of this revivalism was inventive and in excellent taste. Such buildings by Shaw as Baring's Bank in Bishopsgate, Swan House on Chelsea Embankment and 196 Queen's Gate, were not only hugely influential but great works of architecture in themselves. Much of it, on the other hand, was undoubtedly unimaginative and shoddy. Yet it is a style which dominates miles of main street frontages both in the City and Westminster and along the radial routes out of them. Perhaps when people tire of the clinical modernity of so much steel, glass and concrete, it is a style whose restless gables and wealth of detail will find greater favour. But at present, it is a period of British architecture that is shamefully neglected.

With the turn of the twentieth century, the story becomes a profoundly unhappy one. The first half of this century produced virtually nothing which can be considered a credit to the face of London. The brilliance of Shaw vanished into the empty revivalism that followed him. Sir Edwin Lutyens, one of the few good architects of the period, probably did less good by his own works than he did harm by setting a fashion for the neo-Wren and neo-Georgian that is the stamp of so many London buildings today. His contemporaries, such as Sir Aston Webb, Sir Reginald Blomfield and Sir Herbert Baker, whose impact on the present appearance of London is considerably greater than that of Nash or Cubitt, were all competent, but utterly lacking in flair or imagination. Many of the key sites in London—Regent Street, Trafalgar Square, the Bank area—were enervated in their hands. And these alas, are the places so frequented by tourists. They left in their wake a tradition not only of erecting dull buildings but of destroying beautiful ones, which is one of the great tragedies of London's history—greater in many ways than that of the Blitz. These were the years when we lost Berkeley Square, Bloomsbury and Park Lane—and gained instead the Aldwych, Holborn Kingsway and the Embankment.

Only in the last decade has London's architecture begun to recover the style it lost for nearly a century. It was spurred on by the example of the London County Council on the South Bank, and by the new designs demanded by the development of high-rise building. The old City of London has undergone as a result its third and most dramatic increase in scale—and surely its last. Today it contains exciting vistas and contrasts which are undoubtedly an improvement on the boring façades of the past fifty years. The picture farther west, however, is less happy, with the indiscriminate placing of 'point blocks' disastrously affecting areas which still depend for their physical character on the preservation of their Georgian—and even their Victorian—scale. But that is a story to be dealt with later in this book.

At this stage it is important only to point out that this brief sprint through history cannot and should not be appreciated as such on the ground. To look at a London street is to concertina history into one visual impression. History does not matter in this. It is what is here and now that is important: how well each of the component parts of a street fit together; how far a tower block blends with or intrudes into a classical façade; whether a few of individually mediocre buildings can suddenly come alive when seen from a certain angle. I have found since I began looking at London streets that it is a very different experience from viewing particular buildings. It is much more exciting, and it can also be much more frustrating. But it is an experience which I am sure more people should try.

The City

1-Bank

'Bank' used once to be the heart of London. Now this is no longer so. In the geographical centre it may be, but London's heart has moved progressively (or regressively) westwards—to rest at present in Trafalgar Square or Piccadilly Circus. Meanwhile, the old City of London's residential population has declined to less than it was in the Middle Ages and the area round the Bank of England has become more and more true to its name. It has become an area of banks and bankers.

But to anyone standing at the foot of Wellington's statue in front of the Royal Exchange, there is no doubting that this is the centre of something. Eight streets lead off from the area in front of this statue. And each corner is dominated by buildings in a nineteenth- or early twentieth-century style that can only be termed 'classical imposing'. These are indeed the buildings of the heart of empire. And however boring and unimaginative they may seem at first glace, when taken all together in the right atmosphere, their qualities begin to reverberate, building up to a crescendo of massive pillars, giant pediments, colossal entrances and opulent but austere stonework. Indeed, this subtly shaped place (which has no name other than that of its Tube Station, 'Bank') is the architectural epitome of civic importance. It is no coincidence that its style can be found in the centres of other commercial cities such as Manchester, Birmingham, Liverpool and Leeds.

The Royal Exchange building (which many people mistakenly take for the Bank of England itself) is something of a disappointment, especially considering the history of its site. This is the third Royal Exchange and was built in 1844, though it still has the old grasshopper weathervane that was the crest of the founder and

Mansion House.

builder of the first one back in 1565, Sir Thomas Gresham. It is in a ponderous Victorian classical style, with a massive portico topped by a pediment containing a relief representing all sorts of worthy city activities. In it Lady Commerce is supported by the Lord Mayor and Aldermen, a Common Councillor and numerous merchants, while beneath is written, 'The Earth is the Lord's and the Fulness thereof'—which was easy enough to say if you were a Victorian banker.

The interior of the Exchange—which has not been used as such since 1939—was until recently a sadly neglected part of the Guildhall Museum. Now its splendid old floor of rough Turkish hone-stone, relic of a previous Exchange, is even emptier. It is all a stupid waste. What is needed is for some really imaginative city father to get down to making what should be the throbbing heart of the commercial city just that again. Here is the archetypal precinct—spacious, covered and very handsome—in which could be provided all manner of amusements and facilities for City office workers. No one ever went to the museum, but they would flock to a real new 'exchange' of small stalls, cafés and exhibitions—a jumble of commercial and civic activity that was after all the character of the old Exchange. And it could even make someone a handsome profit.

The space in front of the Exchange is already used for occasional displays and exhibitions—frequently adding a touch of the bizarre to the heart of the city. One never quite knows when rounding the corner whether there will be a live cow, a piece of artillery, a famine relief display or a beauty queen sitting incongruously amid all the traffic.

Down to the right of the Royal Exchange runs that warren of streets with fascinating names such as Throgmorton, Threadneedle, Tokenhouse Yard and Austin Friars. Although, like most City streets, they are superficially dull and pompous, they all possess that golden quality: the ability to surprise with occasional flashes of style and quaintness. It is what has made the City the object of perpetual pleasure to the determined sightseer—just as it is neglected utterly by the day-tripper. Look, for instance, down Capel Court off Bartholomew Lane. Here is the old main entrance to the Stock Exchange—Victorian and stuccoed rather like the garden front of a Regency villa, but with the great mass of the new Stock Exchange tower piled up behind it.

To the right of Wellington's statue runs the imposing wall of the Bank of England itself, its main buildings inside stepped back from it like some Peking temple. The Bank was founded back in 1694 to raise money for an impecunious monarch, but it has been successively rebuilt and altered since then, with steadily declining taste. Its greatest incarnation was at the hands of Sir John Soane—one of the most brilliantly original of Georgian architects. His Bank was a succession of walls and domes, secure but light and remarkably modern. All that can be seen of this today is the outer wall. Built in 1801, it is renowned as a masterful solution to the problem of making a high, thick windowless wall—necessary for security—none the less graceful and in tune with surrounding buildings. It has no windows or other apertures, but its line is broken by columns set into bays. The corner opposite the Mansion House is best of all. It could so easily have been an ugly stone prow jutting out into the street. In fact, its perfect pair of Corinthian columns carry the eye round into Prince's Street so easily that one hardly notices there is a corner there at all.

The superstructure inside—interwar by Sir Herbert Baker—is the more disastrous when one remembers what it replaced. Sir Nikolaus Pevsner writes, on the subject of the retention of the outer wall: 'The use of Soane's masterwork as the footstool of a Herbert Baker seems unforgivable, and Soane was the last man to forgive.' Baker's construction, when viewed from the Exchange steps, seems utterly lifeless and without any discernible character. Strangest and saddest of all, its sky-high portico is not even triumphant or grand—as might reasonably have been expected with such a building in such a position.

To be fair, however, Baker did at least present us with his version of the Tivoli Corner in the Bank wall at the junction of Prince's Street and Lothbury—a neat, domed surprise that turns this corner no worse than Soane turned the previous one.

On the corner site of Prince's Street and Poultry stands the National Provincial Bank. Begun in 1929—a strange year to build a bank—it is pompous and without character, full of sharp corners and aggressive details and the more obtrusive for having been cleaned a shining white. Next to it, however, is a much better version of the same in the Midland Bank, by Sir Edwin Lutyens, doyen of the commercial classical style.

Poultry stretches beyond into Cheapside—the old High Street

of the City of London and still containing branches of many big stores. It is one of the City's few really straight streets, leading up to St. Paul's. Its vista, dominated by the striking tower of Wren's St. Mary-le-Bow, gives a dramatic sense of space to the Bank area.

The corner of Poultry and Queen Victoria Street contains a charming Italian-Gothic five-storey building with a turret at the end (or at least it does at present; rumours of demolition). It subtly prevents the streets on either side from seeming like caverns, and though it badly needs a clean it is a delightful relic of the days when the City's architects operated on a more domestic scale.

Queen Victoria Street was substantially damaged in the war and much really bad building has gone up since—too box-like in itself and too prone to a belief that gaping open spaces in between make up for it. Under the circumstances it would have been much better to throw regulation to the winds and leave it to private enterprise to cram everything it could on to the available space.

There is, however, one precious relic which sums up everything there is to say about the present-day City. There, tucked away behind the Mansion House amid towering blocks of concrete, stands—or squats—St. Stephen's Walbrook. Its marvellously ancient rough stone is so human that it might almost be a real person, standing there confronting all that soulless modernity round him. St. Stephen's was Wren's dummy run for St. Paul's—a brilliant experiment with space and light that grew into his own peculiar brand of English Baroque.

St. Stephen's used to be situated on the banks of the Walbrook, the stream that from Roman times to the Middle Ages was the chief watercourse for the City. It has long been covered over, but its moisture did preserve one unique relic discovered during modern excavations—the Roman Temple to Mithras. The temple was dug up and relaid in the forecourt of Temple Court at the top of Queen Victoria Street, supposedly for better public view. It looks bleak and incongruous here and would surely have been better removed to a museum somewhere, where at least it might have been looked at in comfort by those that want to see it. It loses all significance here.

The Mansion House, official residence of the Lord Mayor of London (not of all London, just the old City) sits across the angle to Lombard Street. It is a fine eighteenth-century Palladian classical building by George Dance—one of the very few surviving buildings of its style and period in the City. Like so many of London's official buildings, it is pleasantly domestic in exterior appearance—a particular important quality here, surrounded as it is by so many later and grosser versions of the classical style. Gentle steps lead up to the entrance behind the portico and bulging flower-boxes and trees in tubs make it all the more friendly. In the pediment a relief represents London trampling on Envy and guiding Plenty.

The view down Lombard Street is dominated by Nicholas Hawksmoor's extraordinary church of St. Mary Woolnoth (1716). The church is a magnificent exercise in filling a difficult corner, of which there are so many round this area—this time the one with King William Street. The massive, but always controlled, rustication of the ground floor produces a main body to the building of immense strength and vigour, although the west front is unmistakably that of a church, with the bold features of the ground floor reducing subtly but swifty to two simple small towers. But the most remarkable thing is how well it all blends with the nineteenth-century banking houses on either side. It is almost as if Hawksmoor predicted the boldness and brashness of the City architects of 150 years later and produced a church that he was sure would stand them in good stead.

Lombard Street itself is the very heart of the London banking community—deriving its name dutifully from the bankers of Lombardy who were its precursors in importance. All the eighteenth-century manifestations of its early days have gone, such as the coffee-houses where stocks were exchanged round the table. Now all the buildings are late nineteenth- and early twentieth-century opulence. But the great signs of the banking houses still jut out from the walls as symbols of their past, and as something for schoolchildren to identify.

The Royal Insurance Building, on the corner with Cornhill, completes the circle round the Bank. It is another competent exercise in turning a corner, again in a classical style and enlivened by numerous colourful window-boxes. Farther down Cornhill are more of those blessed City alleyways. Ball Court leads to the famous tavern of Simpsons, and Castle Court beyond it leads to the 'George and Vulture', of Pickwickian fame. In St.

Michael's Alley beyond, apparently, the first London coffee-shop was established when an Arab youth was allowed to sell 'a liquor' from a stall—in 1657.

From the corner of Cornhill the view across the Royal Exchange is already dominated by the new Stock Exchange tower beyond. It is the first intrusion of the twentieth century into an area of the City of London that still manages to epitomise the styles of the nineteenth. It will doubtless not be the last.

St. Paul's and the Choir School from Watling Street.

2-*St. Paul's Precinct*

There is one thing that any amount of modern tower development cannot do to the City of London. It cannot destroy the status of St. Paul's Cathedral as London's greatest single architectural monument. And although height has now become commonplace, St. Paul's is still breath-taking in its impression of towering grandeur, set there on its hill on the west side of the old City.

After its rebuilding, following the Great Fire in 1666, St. Paul's was enclosed by the neat, cosy streets and alleyways of Georgian London. Most of this was superseded by a mass of considerably less cosy Victorian commercial development. Both styles, however, sympathised with the usual appreciation of the cathedral's exterior—a two-tier structure with the main body of nave, transept and twin-porticoed west front taken in scale with surrounding buildings, while the towers and dome should be seen from afar, floating over the rooftops of the post-Great Fire City. This split personality does not always wholly succeed—the two baroque west towers, for instance, sit most strangely on the much more refined and delicate classical west front. But the point is that the buildings in St. Paul's Churchyard adhered to it and respected at least one of the ideas behind Wren's construction.

The Blitz in the last war put paid to most of this. Indeed it was one of the many miracles of that period that it did not put paid to the cathedral itself. Almost all the buildings round it were either destroyed or remained standing in such a position that their retention was pointless. Indeed, most of those to the south side of the cathedral were of little or no architectural significance anyway.

The opportunity was thus offered to do new justice to St. Paul's as had never been offered since the late seventeenth century. To be fair to the City Corporation and the cathedral authorities, they never (except perhaps at the very beginning) failed to acknowledge the importance of this task. Indeed, they were thinking and talking about the practical problems of architectural environment and amenity long before most of their contemporaries on other locations. If they appear now to have failed despite all this, it is at least partly because the forces against them were just too strong; forces not only represented by the pressures of the commercial developers, but also by the architectural fashions and conventional wisdom of the fifties and early sixties—above all, the absolute craze for overall comprehensive development, a craze from which Christopher Wren was himself not free. Perhaps, indeed, the problem of what could ever satisfactorily be placed alongside a building of St. Paul's genius and originality was an insoluble one from the start.

All, however, is by no means lost. Good bits of the area round St. Paul's still survive: some of the new development is very good indeed. And, above all, from almost every angle there are exciting views of the cathedral itself—sometimes developing gradually down the line of a distant street, sometimes suddenly leaping out from a glimpse between two buildings.

The most famous approach to St. Paul's is from the west up Ludgate Hill. Rising from where the old Fleet River once flowed past Ludgate, the view bends gently and then suddenly explodes with the full force of Wren's west front. The siting with relation to the hill looks casually brilliant, the front pointing slightly south of the line of Ludgate Hill. Wren, of course, wanted the new London built after the Fire to be like a good renaissance city—all long avenues and right-angles. But commercial pressures dictated the old pattern, and this view of St. Paul's is one of London's most vivid reminders of the jumbled character of the medieval city. Crucial to this view is the stark, black spire of St. Martin's Ludgate, piling up from Wren's clean white tower in a series of exciting shapes. Even in the softest light, this spire acts as a hard point of focus moving across the view of St. Paul's as the viewer walks towards it down the length of Fleet Street and across into Ludgate Hill. It throws Wren's columns and dome into majestic relief—just as he intended.

Down Warwick Lane, left off Ludgate Hill, lies a solitary remnant of the days when this area was a mass of little streets named after parts of the Lord's Prayer: Amen Court. It is a secluded row of Georgian buildings, opening out into a garden with Victorian houses and a gate-house—all belonging to the cathedral. It is calm and peaceful, almost a provincial cathedral close, and a million miles from the centre of London. To the north is the new precinct in place of old Paternoster Square—once the haunt of London's publishing community. It has all the right things: segregated traffic, massive below-decks parking, pedestrian precinct, with shops and restaurants—and with Lord Holford to design it. It could have been a lot worse, but is that enough for this site?

Juxon House, jutting out to obscure the west front, and the subject of raging controversy when erected, is none-the-less a neat, inoffensive block. The other blocks are well designed and modern without screaming across at the cathedral. The shopping area is also successful in its scale and sense of enclosure, though it is a little angular.

But somehow the whole thing lacks heart. The wide concourse leading to the steps down to the west front is ludicrously big. It is always empty and windswept, with little groups of people huddling round its perimeter beneath lowering buildings. St. Paul's was never intended to be in acres of clinical concrete. It should build up its crescendo from a jumble of buildings and small streets—a layout which could have achieved the same density without losing a human scale.

However, if the Paternoster Square development was a brave attempt to do right by St. Paul's, the renewal of the area to the east has been a disaster. The corner of Cheapside, once one of London's most famous cross-roads, is now a mess. And the new Bank of England development in boring neo-Georgian red brick is as wretched an example of non-planning as can be found anywhere in London. Farther round across Watling Street is the equally appalling development for Wiggins Teape. It is hard to imagine that anyone can have looked at the plans for this building, back in the fifties, with any thought of St. Paul's in his mind at all. It has a particularly vulgar coloured frieze running round it.

Wiggins Teap gazes across Cannon Street, however, at the extraordinary *Financial Times* building, Bracken House. Built by Sir Albert Richardson in 1959—though who could have guessed that date?—it is the sort of building that most people regard as lovably hideous. Undoubtedly its most memorable feature is its red sandstone and brown brick covering. It is at least a bold beacon of character in an area that is bidding fair to becoming the most soulless in the whole City.

The eastern approach to St. Paul's is, however, redeemed by two things. The superb new buildings for St. Paul's Choir School, set in gardens immediately beneath the apse, act as a brilliant foil to Wren's architecture. To prove the point, they incorporate the surviving (but reconstructed) spire of Wren's St. Augustine's Church. Divided into deceptively diminutive blocks, they are dutifully humble against the splendid baroque of the east front. Yet the projecting, lead-covered attic storey, which provides a bold horizontal line, allows the composition to make itself vigorously felt on its own. Wren would certainly have approved.

And behind it, down Watling Street beside the horrors of the Bank of England, can be had the best view of St. Paul's of all. The tower of St. Augustine's, the choir school and then above them the dome, south transept and west tower of the cathedral pile up on one another—not sedate as in more conventional views, but full of excitement and movement. This is the true baroque. The street opens out into a small garden just south of the choir school, with a fountain and surrounding trees which give it, at least potentially, an almost cloistered seclusion. It is the best place in which to relax and view St. Paul's from its finest angle.

The south side of the precinct area is dominated by the modern wastelands of Old Change Court, an 'open space' which antecedes the north side precinct in every way. It is extraordinary that anyone could have conceived this wide, windswept area as enhancing the view of the cathedral. It is merely an excuse for some massive, characterless blocks, in concrete already stained and dirty, which it only serves to make more obtrusive.

Beyond it, however, is a good approach up Peter's Hill. It is hoped one day that these steps may run right up from the river. At present they climb—always with the south transept looming ahead—past the College of Heralds in Queen Victoria Street, with the charming old Sermon Lane on the left. The steps finally open out into a suitably restrained piazza with well-designed seats, balustrades and flower-boxes. It deserves full marks for simply not being too big.

Finally, to the south-west of the cathedral lies the great opportunity. This must be one of the last areas of the City still awaiting post-war development. But first, two buildings of real importance lie buried within it. The old Deanery of St. Paul's is a magnificent late seventeenth-century house believed to have been built by Wren himself, and tucked away between tall Victorian blocks down Dean Court. And Apothecaries' Hall, even harder to find, is down Carter Lane towards Blackfriars. It is a superb enclosed guildhall, dating from the seventeenth century but with Georgian refacing, and with a fine doorway and delightfully peaceful little courtyard inside. Apart from these museum pieces, the area possesses one quality which must above all be retained in any redevelopment. This quality lies in the maze of small streets, squares and alleyways—such as Bell Yard, Wardrobe Place and St. Andrew's Hill—that lead off the main through street, Carter Lane. The buildings in these by-ways may be mostly Victorian and dirty—though that is not their fault—but they are small-scale and intimate both individually and in their predominantly medieval layout. Even if it is impossible to preserve them in their present form—and that is by no means proven—it is essential that their character be re-created, however modern the style. For it is the character which still exists farther east in the streets round Bishopsgate and which has been all but lost from the area of St. Paul's and Queen Victoria Street. No one wants vast open spaces and concourses here; the blocks can be crammed into whatever density is desired, just so long as these oases remain or are re-created. And if the City Corporation want to see it done well, they need only look at Brighton Square, in the Lanes in Brighton, or at Reporton Road in Fulham. High density and human scale are not necessarily mutually exclusive.

St. Giles Precinct in the Barbican

3-Barbican

Depending on the direction from which you approach it, it can explode upon you suddenly, build up gradually from a series of glimpses, or merely intrude upon some other, more sedate vista.

The Barbican scheme in the City is undoubtedly the most impressive and self-confident piece of urban redevelopment undertaken in Britain since the war. It is the product of ideas way in advance of the sterile, post-Blitz design of cities such as Plymouth, or even more advanced conceptions such as Coventry or Birmingham. It is rooted firmly in the principle that working, playing and living are all integral parts of a vital city centre, and it will accommodate enough people to double the City's night-time population. So far, so good.

The scheme is not yet complete and has not yet begun to work properly. However, as a planning exercise it is already showing defects that will be hard to rectify. Planners still find it hard to recognise that people like to walk on the ground. The first-floor walkways on which the whole scheme is based are uninviting and windswept. Many of the shop sites have yet to be let but those that have look desolate. There is no action, no friendliness up there in the air, and there is always the feeling of just filling in the gaps between the office blocks. No wonder so many people still use the pavements of the streets below.

Farther over, the area devoted to residential use has yet to be completed. But already the sheer massiveness of it all is overpowering. Great cliffs enclose the central garden area, with three huge towers soaring over them. Trees will, of course, make a big difference. But the blocks will remain brutal rather than homely—something of a latter-day Dolphin Square.

In purely architectural terms, however, if such terms exist, the

Barbican is a magnificent achievement. The best approach to it is from the Guildhall area to the south. And here, by way of contrast, is fortuitous city planning at its best. What other city would have its seat of government in such a cosy corner as Guildhall Yard? It is surrounded by the eighteenth century Gothic façade of the Hall, Wren's St. Lawrence Jewry Church, the old Georgian court house, the Irish Chamber and a fine Palladian screen. Sadly the City Corporation, so emboldened by their grandiose doings to the north, want to tear most of it down and create more space. Space, that menace of so much post-war town planning, is the last thing this corner needs.

From the back of Guidhall, steps lead up past the modern Guildhall Museum and over London Wall, known as Route 11. From the bridge the grandeur of the Barbican becomes apparent.

Six large rectangular office blocks are set obliquely to the road, three on each side, with lesser blocks scattered round their bases. These blocks form the commercial and architectural spine of the development. They are smart, if unimaginative, and should wear well. Their chief defect is that they will soon doubtless look too short.

Beyond them, to the north-east, rises the much higher Britannic House. It is in smokey green glass—cool and sophisticated and the finest skyscraper to date in London. The entrance in Moor Lane is sunk slightly, making the height more sheer. The main aluminium vertical strips are offset by more slender alternate ones and then by narrow strips of window-frame, all going the complete height uninterrupted. For glaring contrast, the new concrete fire station opposite is as clear an example of architecture's brutalist tradition as Britannic House is of its refined classical one.

Buried behind the series ranks of Route 11 lie the asides, so typically London and so mercifully reproduced in a way that no other country might have attempted. Sudden jutting sections of Roman Wall are set in small gardens, trees and flowers poke their way into the most soulless view and, most curious of all, there is the new Barber Surgeon's Hall in Monkwell Square. This building is almost a visual joke, so incongruous is its reproduction early-Georgian style against all the modernity—but a sad joke in that good Georgian should have been spoiled by two attics which destroy the effect of the front pediment. However, it is a refreshing memorial to a style to which London owes much and which makes even the surrounding steel and glass curtain-walling seem sympathetic. Monkwell Square, incidentally, admirably illustrates the point about being on the ground. Grass and trees and street-lamps and old-fashioned architecture seem to belong there. From up above on the surrounding first-floor walkway, they look substantial and real. To be up there looking down is to feel out-of-place and insecure. Psychologically, people just do not like walking in the air, to be swept by planners and architects from one subtle level to another. This surely is the Barbican's biggest mistake.

To the north of the Square is the new City of London Girls' School. This is excellent. Carefully controlled panels of brick and glass draw the line of the building down to the ground, making it look two storeys instead of four. It is just the right scale for this development and it is in just the right place.

Over the top, still in harmony, peeps the tower of St. Giles Cripplegate beyond, sole survivor (apart from the Roman Wall) of the pre-Blitz Barbican. The church itself has been set in a tiled preinct with the school buildings round it. Old-style lamps and benches have been scattered here and there across the precinct adding just the right touch of period elegance.

This is the heart of the Barbican. From it, the whole conception is clear and the tiles and the marvellous old late-Gothic church give it a warmth and an intimacy lacking in either the colossal flats to the north or the geometrical office blocks along Route 11 It is modern urban design at its best. But here again something is wrong, not architecturally but sociologically. Here in the heart of the whole development was surely not the place to put nothing but an Anglican Church and a single-sex girls' grammar school. For once, we are on the ground, not up in the air. This is precisely where there should be masses of people for as much of the time as possible. Here should be the shops, pubs, restaurants and the entrance to a Tube Station. With the balcony overlooking the lake towards the Arts Centre, it would have made one of the most attractive High Streets in London. As it is, someone has blundered.

Back, however, to the architecture. At the time of writing the predominantly residential area to the north was still a massive building site. But the chief buildings were already sufficiently complete to give a good idea of the outline of the scheme. Architecturally, their impact is immense. The strong horizontal line of the terrace blocks, occasionally perched on massive columns over the central garden area, is balanced by the soaring vertical sky-scrapers. The towers, designed by the architects Chamberlin, Powell and Bon, are the most daring features of the whole scheme. They are triangular in shape with bold gondola-like balconies on each corner right the way up. They will be the tallest residential blocks in Europe, and round their base will be grouped an arts centre and a theatre leading down to an ornamental lake. The danger of it all becoming too precious is alleviated by the sheer scale. Viewed at night from St. Giles' precinct, it looks like some vast creation of town-planners' science fiction.

It would be unfair at this stage to judge whether such monumental twentieth-century architecture can none-the-less provide a tolerable environment for humans to live in. Deprived of landscaping it is certainly an overpowering experience, patently in danger of suffering from the soullessness of the not dissimilar Parkhill estate in Sheffield. Undoubtedly it suffers from the faults of blandness and lack of variety that afflicts so much post-war comprehensive redevelopment—excusable perhaps where the buildings are commercial, but less so where people have to live with them all the time. However, the Barbican is a bold attempt to reverse the natural depopulation of the city centre—so bold it deserves more praise than it has so far received. One can only hope that when that exercise is repeated elsewhere—at Covent Garden and St. Katherine's Docks—the lessons of the Barbican will have been well learnt.

4-Bishopsgate

Bishopsgate is one of the great old streets of London. It formed the chief route through the Roman city from the river crossing northwards. In medieval times it contained a number of fine mansions—including the magnificent Crosby Hall, belonging to Sir John Crosby, which has been re-erected in Cheyne Walk, Chelsea. The old Gate itself, frequently rebuilt, was finally demolished in 1761. Today, apart from the churches, nothing of the medieval street remains, and precious little even from the eighteenth century.

Until recently, Bishopsgate was essentially a nineteenth-century and commercial street, its architecture typifying the pride and self-confidence of the Victorian merchants and bankers—particularly the latter. Today, however, even their towering palaces are being overshadowed, as a succession of skyscraper developments sprout on or near its line. Bishopsgate is now struggling, as it always has struggled, to maintain its position as the City's backbone in the new age of 'high-rise'.

The impact of the new towers is drastic—far greater than was the impact of the Victorians on the earlier Georgian street. Where previously its line—the line of the roofs, cornices and fenestration—was inched up gradually with each new building, today it can be suddenly dwarfed by a high building which may not even be particularly near it. However much this intrusion may be deplored farther west, it would be futile to try to cry halt to such development in the City. Soaring land prices would make a nonsense even of Victorian-sized buildings and the City can fairly claim that it either expands or dies—or swamps the West End, which would have, and is already having, its own disadvantages. The important thing now is to protect at all costs those corners of streets such as

St. Ethelburga's Church, Bishopsgate.

Bishopsgate that still embody the unique character of the City and allow, indeed encourage, really exciting and substantial redevelopment to high densities over the rest. Indeed the saddest thing about the City is not the destruction of its Victorian scale—that was inevitable—but the fact that it has been destroyed by so many measly, half-hearted buildings.

Bishopsgate really begins at the massive Guardian Assurance Building that first greets the traveller from the south across London Bridge—although here it is called Gracechurch Street (after grass, not grace). This building is about as dull as you can get, an utterly unmemorable blend of various styles, culminating in a curious red-tiled roof. What a welcome to the City!

Gracechurch Street swings to the right of it, and immediately the new City is evident in the tower of Barclays Bank ahead. First, however, it is the old that should get a glance, down Fish Street. Here Wren's Monument rises in memory of the Great Fire of London, which broke out in a neighbouring lane. It is a remarkably fine column on a square plinth with a square balcony on top offering an excellent view of the City to those able and willing to climb the steps. The view is all the better for not being too high, such that other spires and modern towers are thrown into relief rather than dwarfed. Round the base of the Monument are weather-worn reliefs, depicting the King offering relief to the City while workmen go about rebuilding it.

The junction with Fenchurch Street is dominated by the new Barclays Tower—not a particularly exciting one, too squat and clad in concrete that will, on past experience, weather badly. Down Fenchurch Street to the right, however, is the much smarter new tower of the Kleinwort Benson building.

Farther up Gracechurch Street, a turning on the right down Bull's Head Passage leads into the back of Leadenhall Market. It is a quite extraordinary survival—almost a Casbah in comparison with the commercial sobriety of the main streets round about it. Small alleys wind in and out, packed with shops, until they plunge into the towering Victorian Hall of the market itself. This is a splendid iron-vaulted maroon-and-cream creation of 1881 in a cruciform shape, the east wing being turned slightly to the south providing an exciting perspective. The eerie light from the vaulting overhead, the friendly stalls, the ornate ironwork and the general liveliness that goes into any market is just the refreshing atmosphere the City needs at this point. In its casual way, the City wins again.

Coming out of the market into Gracechurch Street, provided the light is right, the neo-Dutch gabling on its main entrance can be seen exotically reflected in the plate-glass windows of the Guinness Mahon building opposite. The entrance to this building, carefully set obliquely to the street, is excellent—neatly designed and well proportioned. It is modern commercial office-building at its best.

Almost next door, the shops stop suddenly and there is a blank wall. On it is written the bald name, St. Peter's Cornhill. Above, however, can be seen the five plain east windows of this church, whose entrance is round in Cornhill. And above those five are three more, set into a gable, one round-headed, the other two circular. It is delightful and ingenious, further evidence if any were needed of Christopher Wren's endless inventiveness.

Ahead at the junction with Cornhill is the actual start of Bishopsgate proper, starting with some good examples of nineteenth-century commercial architecture. On the right is a palazzo for the Belgian Bank—suitably French in detailing, especially on the top storey. Beyond that is a surprisingly domestic building by Norman Shaw for Baring Bros.—in a free Queen Anne style with, of all things in the City, red brick and white woodwork. It has a fine iron lantern over the doorway.

Turning the kink in Bishopsgate ahead is the great single-storey National Provincial Bank, strongly reminiscent of Soane's wall round the Bank of England, built roughly half a century earlier. It was built by an architect named Gibson in 1865 and has all the aggression and flair of the mid-Victorian period. The tall windows are arched and separated by columns, and the massive doorway on the corner has a grand plaque set over it. The top is decorated by florid statuary. It all longs for the clean that should come when the entire site behind is redeveloped by the new National Westminster Bank, to include a handsome 600-foot tower by Richard Seifert.

Handsome tower, maybe. But what will happen to an architectural gem situated on the far side of the site down Old Broad Street? The City of London Club might be a straightforward transplant from Pall Mall, complete with stuccoed exterior. It comes as a ray of sunshine on this pleasant curve in Old Broad

Street down to the new Stock Exchange tower. The classical style, by Philip Hardwick, is slightly heavier than might have been the case had Nash or Decimus Burton had a hand in it up West. The swags under the porch and the solid cornice are decidedly Victorian rather than Regency. But the basis is still Palladian, with pilasters and fine first-floor windows. But can it survive its threatened and quite unnecessary extinction by the National Westminster rebuilding behind?

Back in Bishopsgate, the commercial architecture becomes less exciting as the street gets wider and the buildings lower, depriving them of some of their earlier drama. Most of the fun now is hidden. A tiny alley on the right leads down to Great St. Helen's. Here a row of houses, not originals but just the right Georgian scale, surround a small courtyard. And beyond it sits the exquisite Church of St. Helen's. It was once attached to a nunnery, giving it its curious twin-aisled appearance, creating a delightful undulating crenellation along the roof, with a small white wooden lantern tower rising from the middle. In front is a garden with trees.

But this is only half the point. The other half rises magnificently to the right—the superb mass of the Commercial Union tower. The juxtaposition of St. Helen's and this huge smokey-glass curtain wall must be one of the most dramatic contrasts of old and new architecture to be found anywhere. Everything about them is exactly opposite—the form, the materials, the details, the scale (to put it mildly) and the purpose. Yet both have a sort of perfection and certainly add tremendous character to one another. If this is the London of the future, then we can rest content.

Farther on up Bishopsgate, on the same side, two massive Tuscan columns herald the entrance to St. Helen's Place—a curiously French cul-de-sac. Although the block at the far end is sufficiently 'camp' to be amusing, it is still amazing how on earth twentieth-century architecture could make sophisticated classical motifs seem so cold and brutal.

Just beyond St. Helen's Place comes the west front of tiny St. Ethelburga's Church, which can only be called quaint. It is sandwiched between two large blocks in so extraordinary a fashion that it almost requires two looks to see it is there. The front of the church used to be covered with old shops, until the street was widened between the wars. Wormwood Street across on the left marks the approximate spot where the old Bishopsgate used to cross the road—hence the name of the church just beyond, St. Botolph Without. This was rebuilt in about 1725 and has a square tower crowned by a cupola. On the other side of its comparatively spacious—and in this area very welcome—garden is a delightful early nineteenth-century school-house with brightly painted figures of a boy and girl in front. The building is now the hall of the Fan Makers' Company.

Next to St. Botolph's and turning the corner to Liverpool Street are two excellent stucco-fronted town houses, presumably early Victorian, making a sober contrast to the romanticism of the Great Eastern Hotel across the way. And here if ever is a building that needs to be cleaned if it is to be properly appreciated. The frontage on to Bishopsgate is a great pile of neo-Dutch-Renaissance. Two pinnacled gables cap each corner of the roof, while the façade is rich with red brick motifs. The only slight eyesore is the entrance to the Abercorn Rooms in the centre, which is rather spoiled by the addition of a jutting semicircular canopy.

Beyond comes Liverpool Street Station itself, a brilliant exercise in Victorian functional architecture inside, and not without decorative interest, however impractical it may all be to travellers. But the long, low exterior line of the roof stretching up Bishopsgate, fronted by single-storey shops, seems to have been the kiss of death. The street suddenly changes completely and dramatically from the grand to the slummy. Gone is the big City opulence. Here is run-down Cockney with a vengeance—cheap stores and seedy alleyways. It is almost as if one has boarded a train at Liverpool Street and gone somewhere else, rather than simply walked a few paces past it. On the right-hand side of the road, the Bishopsgate Institute is still worth a glance—grotesque terracotta with twin towers and a large Flemish arch over the door. By Harrison Townsend, it looks wonderfully absurd among the plain shopfronts, like a grossly over-painted lady in a cheap café.

Down behind it, however, Bishopsgate gives its final fling. There in Spitalfields is an area that must be the saddest survivor of glorious days gone by. It is the most spacious, and dejected, of the great London markets. And beyond it is Hawksmoor's brilliant Christ Church, Spitalfields. Here English baroque is no longer genteel but massive and vigorous; yet today it is in a most depressing state, like a great actor without a part to play. Behind in Fournier Street and Artillery Lane are the fine early-Georgian houses and shops of the cloth merchants who once made this one of the most fashionable parts of town. They are still there, the splendid doorways and porches—just like those in Queen Anne's Gate—but they have almost fallen apart. The victims now of multi-occupation and long the haunts of London's down-and-outs, they cry out, as do their inhabitants, for solutions that have still proved impossible to find.

It is hard not to wonder, as one walks back to the teeming traffic of Bishopsgate, is there no one down the other end of that street that can do something for Spitalfields?

Smithfield Market.

5-Smithfield

Smithfield meat market is spread out on the north-western edge of the old City of London, above what was once the Fleet River and is now Farringdon Road. With its neighbours, sombre Old Bailey and the imposing St. Bartholomew's Hospital, it ought by rights to be one of London's more gruesome quarters. Yet it is nothing of the sort. Indeed, its bustling life and curiously mixed population of porters, nurses and office workers give it an atmosphere that could hardly be more friendly.

The market itself is a priceless Victorian composition. Meat has been bought and sold on its site since the Middle Ages, the streets of west London being even more jammed than they are now by herds of cattle and flocks of sheep being driven to market. The present building must be among the most extensive in the City. It was built in 1866 by a little-known architect, Sir Horace Jones, and is Victorian commercial architecture at its most successful.

It has four quaint octagonal towers at each corner and a magnificent arched colonnade through the middle. The walls consist of bays of stone arches with stone pilasters in between—filled with red brickwork and superb wrought-iron. The central arches themselves are capped by a pediment flanked by ferocious bronze dragons breathing realistic darts of fire down towards the meat passing below. The colonnade itself is again in iron, with excellent railings and ranks of old gas-lamps on brackets on the walls. Perhaps the one sad thing about the market building is the ghastly plastic canopy which surrounds its outside, spoiling the line of the arches and obscuring the view of the ironwork.

The streets off the market have preserved their character remarkably well, perhaps by virtue of their continuous association with the meat trade. Streets such as St. John Street, Charterhouse

Street and Long Lane, although they are largely Victorian in date, are Victorian at its best—small but highly individualistic houses in an endless variety of classical, gothic and Dutch styles, with a few Georgian survivals still among them. St. John Street derives its name from the Priory of the Order of St. John of Jerusalem, which used to stand like so many similar establishments outside the walls of the medieval city. A short walk up it and on the left is the ancient gate of the Priory, still standing and straddling a side-street.

To the north-east of the market, up another sedate Georgian-cum-Victorian street, lies the old Charterhouse, situated across a small leafy square and overshadowed by gaunt Victorian offices. This was a massively important set of historic buildings, devastated by bombing. They have been excellently restored, but are extremely difficult to get in to see. When London's better-known tourist monuments reach saturation point, the authorities could do worse than encourage the governors to put Charterhouse on some of the circuits—relieving the pressure elsewhere, gaining themselves some revenue and allowing more of the world to see their superb architectural treasures.

Back in Smithfield and facing the market across the pleasant green of West Smithfield is St. Bartholomew's Hospital. It is the only surviving hospital in the City and is certainly its largest institution. It was founded in the twelfth century, but the present buildings mostly date from 1732 or later.

The main courtyard was designed by James Gibbs, architect of St. Martin-in-the-Fields—the similarity can best be seen in the rusticated 'Gibbs' windows. It is rather severely classical, not unlike a university court, with bold, solid blocks on each side. However, in this case, the rather weak corners give glimpses of inevitably jarring modern blocks behind.

In the forecourt stands what must be one of the most extraordinary churches in London—the hospital church of St. Bartholomew-the-Less. The tower is medieval, but the most curious feature is an octagonal tower pushing up through the roof of the nave. This was designed by the ingenious George Dance in 1787 and rebuilt in the nineteenth century by Philip Hardwick. Strangest of all are the pointed windows of the octagon with geometrical tracery, peeping over the roof level of the nave.

The pride of the Hospital, however, is its front on to West

Smithfield. The gatehouse was built in 1702, earlier than the main court, and is now being gloriously cleaned. It is a magnificent example of English baroque style, with giant pilasters, a broken pediment and a delightful niche containing a statue of Henry VIII. The Hospital's walls along West Smithfield were built at the same time and are beautifully modulated, with successively a screen of pillars, rusticated arches and ironwork. They are marred only by a wretched projecting canopy running half their length to supply shelter, light and heat to those seated on the benches below. Could these seats really not have been placed elsewhere?

The real gem of Smithfield, however, is the old church of St. Bartholomew-the-Great. With the chapel in the Tower of London, it is the only surviving Norman Church in London. It is approached through a thirteenth-century Gothic archway on the east side of the square, surmounted by a lovely Tudor half-timber gatehouse. The arch itself once formed the entrance to the south aisle of the old Augustinian priory church (yet another priory on this side of the City). Little of the priory remains—indeed its nave is now a peaceful garden and its cloister a children's play-space. The exterior of the present church is almost entirely a late nineteenth-century rebuilding by Sir Aston Webb, although the pleasant brick tower is early seventeenth century, with a lantern on top of it, typical of that time.

The interior, however, makes it one of London's most fascinating buildings—a honeycomb of unexpected corners and chapels dating from almost every century. There are tremendously powerful Norman columns in the nave, with gothic windows above them; there is a pretty little Perpendicular oratory window set high in one of the walls; there are splendid monuments, and one quiet colonnade of the old cloister still standing. It is all a marvellous church and far too little known.

Down beside the church runs Cloth Fair, taking its name from the old wool market that used to be situated there. It contains some excellent small houses demonstrating perfectly just how graceful life in the late seventeenth-century London must have been. Nos. 41–2 are rare surviving examples of Jacobean domestic architecture, built before the Great Fire and before restrictions were placed on such inflammable projecting woodwork. The fine rectangular oriel windows jut out over the pavement, drawing light into rooms that might otherwise be overshadowed by buildings opposite. In the plainer, Georgian No. 43, which has an intriguing false window painted on to its wall, lives that great exponent of Victorian architecture, Sir John Betjeman. Could he not be demonstrating by his environment where his true architectural sympathies lie?

Holborn

6-Holborn

Poor old Holborn never really made it. While the crowded and prosperous Strand, farther south, saw the throngs of travellers moving between the City and the affairs of Church and State at Westminster, the old road to Uxbridge and the west had to make do with a bit of commerce and the army. Holborn Bar—one of the toll-bars erected outside the walls for taxation and defensive purposes—never achieved the fame or the glamour of Temple Bar. And executions were its chief stock-in-trade.

The modern Holborn is, in fact, a very short street, connecting High Holborn with Holborn Viaduct—which flies over the course of the old Fleet River and into the City proper. But it forms a crucial traffic link in the great chain from Marble Arch to St. Paul's, and between the foot of Gray's Inn Road and Holborn Circus it achieves a remarkable and little-recognised sense of 'place'.

Architecturally speaking, it is superficially unexceptionable. But it has some exciting views and a few priceless gems tucked away—London fashion—in most unlikely corners. To the west stretch the soulless caverns of High Holborn and Oxford Street, one of the many major planning blunders of post-war London. The start of Holborn proper, however, is dominated by the great new building for the National Westminster Bank. Replacing, to the Bank's eternal discredit, a literally fabulous late-Victorian terracotta pile of immense originality, the new block is none-the-less one of the more imaginative and unconventional pieces of modern office infilling in central London. The Holborn façade has strong horizontal bands of concrete which are zigzagged in and out to break the line of the frontage and attune, in so far as is remotely possible, with the restlessness of the Tudor buildings

Staple Inn, Holborn.

next door. To this extent the building must be considered a success. It maintains the sense of space in this curious area, enclosing the pavement concourse and holding the eye. It could so easily have created a brutally straight flatness which would have drifted off towards the characterlessness of High Holborn. As it is, it clearly wants to be a part of Holborn proper. But the old trouble is here as before. For while the form is excellent, the materials, the detailed content of the building, fails. The horizontal emphasis may be bold, but it is also much too harsh. The mosaic facing on the underside of the concrete bands is ugly. And the ground floor is hard, uninviting and too heavy—using unattractive materials such as white tiling to clad the thick pillars. Still, it could have been much worse.

Down the alley behind it, however, is the perfect London scene. A small garden overlooked by the Bank building on one side, gives through into a little Georgian courtyard, containing cobbles, a tree and seats. Staple Inn was once one of the Inns of Court and it still has its old sixteenth-century hall, rebuilt after extensive war damage. The main court was eighteenth century but has been necessarily reconstructed since the war. It was here, in the peace and calm behind Holborn, that Dr. Johnson worked for a while.

There is nothing, however, to prepare one for the view of the other side of the north range on to Holborn—apart from the sheer familiarity of the building. For this side of Staple Inn is by far the most remarkable example of extensive Tudor timber-framing still standing in London—although the tiny Temple gatehouse may be more exotic. It is complete with crazy roof-line, steep gables, overhanging oriel windows and warm, inviting shops on the ground floor. Sitting where it does, at the end of Gray's Inn Road and at the beginning of the sweep down to Holborn Circus, it has a superb effect on its neighbourhood. It brings the whole area down to a human size—even the National Westminster along the way. Its casual personality should be scrupulously studied by young architects, for it is one that has gone from modern building.

The view down Holborn from the opposite side from Staple Inn is now dominated by the *Daily Mirror* building—a characterless slab of concrete and glass with bands of particularly vulgar red. Its great wall of concrete dives straight down into the pavement, failing utterly to create whatever impression it was supposed to, and turning this vital corner of Holborn Circus into a windswept undercliff walk. Against it, even the boring neo-Georgian of Thavies Inn beyond it (and was neo-Georgian ever more boring than this?) acquires a certain warmth and humanity.

Back, however, on the north side of Holborn is what the Victorians did when they wanted to build a real monument to corporate pride—the Prudential Assurance Building. Its vivid red Gothic outline has made it one of the best-known Victorian buildings in London. Yet it does somehow fail to inspire as much as a good Gothic building should. Like so many works by its architect, the strange Alfred Waterhouse, it seems too academic to have acquired real feeling. None-the-less, it is thoroughly competent. It has a pleasing consistency about it, with serried ranks of black-tiled turrets and pointed chimneys on the roof, and the ground floor is in particularly exotic tiles and sumptuous marble. True to the assurance principle, the 'Pru' was clearly designed to convince depositors that it would last their lifetimes. To that extent it has certainly done them proud. By contrast, Gamages next door is a disjointed set of late-Victorian buildings in which it is remarkably difficult to detect any architectural merit.

Holborn Circus ahead, however, is a strange success. The traffic gushing out of six side streets never quite dominates the pedestrians, partly because the Circus is a spacious one and there is a lot of pavement, partly also because the cars are forced to make extraordinary contortions to round the absurd statue of Prince Albert in the centre: a statue which has been dubbed 'the most idiotic in London'. The Prince is looking improbably buccaneering astride a horse and waving his hat in the air.

Leading north from the Circus runs Hatton Garden—named from the time when the Holborn area was fertile with market-gardens leading down to the banks of the Fleet River. The building on the corner has recently been cleaned, turning a dull late Victorian block into a gleaming soft-stone beacon. What a difference it makes to the whole feel of the Circus!

Hatton Garden is a mixture of Georgian and later houses, now mostly housing the diamond and jewellery trade and with some delightful old shop-fronts. A tiny alley on the right goes down past the ancient Mitre Tavern which, with Ely Place beyond, is a relic of the days when this was the London estate of the Bishop of Ely. Ely Place is a totally secluded row of late eighteenth-century houses still private and with a gatehouse. It is still officially excluded from police jurisdiction.

Down among the houses on the left side stands the old chapel belonging to the original palace, St. Etheldreda's—a superb early-Gothic survival with Decorated style tracery. The church reverted to the Roman Catholics in the nineteenth century—a rare occurrence—and has some excellent statues of Catholic martyrs on the walls. It also has numerous other grim reminders of the religious atrocities that took place against the Catholics just outside in Holborn.

Farther round Holborn Circus, Charterhouse Street gives a dramatic side-view of Smithfield market in the distance. And directly east runs the extraordinary Holborn Viaduct. Before the nineteenth century, the road here dipped right down into the 'valley' of the Fleet, with St. Andrew's Church on an eminence by the Circus. Now the street hardly deigns to recognise that it is passing over a river-bed and entering the ancient City of London. It flies over with only four well-restored Victorian statues on the parapet to catch the eye, making straight for the sombre Old Bailey ahead.

On the near side of the Viaduct rises the City Temple, a good example of nineteenth-century classical architecture with a fine portico and a remarkably restrained baroque tower—considering its date (1873). Curiously, while the High Church Anglicans were experimenting with the Gothic revival, it was the nonconformists, at the City Temple and at many Free Church chapels, who remained firmly in the Georgian tradition. Indeed, here the tower and dome are worthy of the age of Wren. They have recently been carefully restored after bomb damage.

But for the real Wren it is only necessary to go next door to St. Andrew's. Here, for once, the authorities have done him proud. Where old and scruffy warehouses previously blotted out its west front, there is now a neat garden with seats.

The effect of demolishing the warehouses has been to open up the view of the whole church right across Holborn Circus, to which, cleaned and white, it adds an invaluable touch of homely style. The tower is the old one of the previous Gothic church and an original Gothic window appears above the west door. The rest, however, is vintage Wren—in renaissance rather than English baroque style. The windows are round-headed with clear glass in them, and the east front on to Shoe Lane has a large Venetian window.

The story of the treatment accorded St. Andrew's has been a thoroughly happy one. May its success be applied elsewhere.

7-Fleet Street

Fleet Street used to be the main route from the old City of London out across the Fleet River through the Ludgate and on towards the Strand and Westminster. It became, first and foremost, the district where lawyers lived, wined and dined, half-way between the commercial centre of the City and the Courts at Westminster where they practised. They still do today (see Chapter 9) and the two Temples still lend two buildings of immense value to the western end of the Street. But Fleet Street is now primarily a street of newspapers, and its architecture reflects this fact. And since newspapers are self-important institutions with very definite ideas of their own image, their architecture can be expected to have character, it not necessarily quality.

The unfortunate thing about the Fleet Street papers is that they mostly developed in the course of the twentieth century, eating up the buildings that had gone before and erecting in their place ones that were inevitably based in the design tradition of their day. For the most part, the period just before and after the first world war was not the most distinguished one in the history of British architecture, though it was still capable of coming up with a few surprises.

Fleet Street begins at Ludgate Circus—however much people may usually approach it from the other end. Here is the great approach to St. Paul's up Ludgate Hill, an approach which dominates Fleet Street along its entire length. Indeed, the gradually exploding view of its dome, towers and portico, with St. Martin's Ludgate in the foreground, especially in a soft morning or evening light, must surely be one of the finest sights in Europe. If ever there was a sign needed that the small-scale prettiness of the West End was behind and the real City was here in earnest, this is it.

The Daily Express building, Fleet Street.

St. Paul's is undoubtedly Fleet Street's most important architectural feature.

And it has another which is still nothing to do with the Press. Fleet Street ran through the heart of the first of London's suburbs outside the old walls. As such, it is basically medieval in character—its curving line alone shows that. And this meant that it was crossed by a maze of small streets and alleyways, often leading to tiny squares. Since this area lay outside the sweep of destruction caused by the Great Fire of London—and the comprehensive rebuilding that followed it—it was able to retain most of these through the centuries. All were rebuilt at some time or another, each time to a larger scale, but they still survive—usually in the form of little passages through the façades of buildings on the main street. Sadly, only a handful of even the seventeenth- and eighteenth-century buildings remain. And the reconstruction that has taken place since the widespread bomb damage of the last war has been almost universally soulless. The sites were too valuable to wait for a good architect to come along. The result is now often pathetic passages between towering walls—which would have been much better obliterated altogether.

An example of what once was, however, can be seen in Racquet Court, on the right just up from Ludgate Circus. Some charmingly old-fashioned shop-fronts lead through to a small court at the end of which stands No. 5, possibly late seventeenth-century and a prosperous five-bays wide. It has a sumptuously ornate door-hood.

Back to Fleet Street and down St. Bride's Avenue is another relic of an earlier age—the wedding-cake spire of Wren's St. Bride's Church. Especially from close to, it piles up magnificently into the sky, rising sheer out of the encircling buildings. It must be the most cramped church in London and it is quite impossible to gain an impression of it as a whole. But, as Wren understood so well, it is the surprise view, the sudden dramatic glimpse that makes the impact.

Beyond St. Bride's begins newspaper-land with a vengeance, with Beaverbrook Newspapers' *Daily Express* building. This is much the liveliest and best of the Fleet Street blocks, with all the brash sensationalism of its inmates. It was erected back in the 1930s by an exuberant Lord Beaverbrook and was intended to be the last word in modern design. (As such it can be compared with Peter Jones in Chelsea of much the same date.) By the firm of

Ellis & Clarke, it is a totally unconventional building in the Bauhaus tradition. It is faced in shiny black sections, with horizontal bands of continuous windows, which even turn round the curved corners—a favourite inter-war gimmick. Viewed today it has a strangely dated air about it—the stepped roof-line and the mock cornice would certainly be scorned by modern curtain-wallers. And its entrance and front hall have to be seen to be believed for their riot of pre-war motifs; it might be the set for an early talkie. But none-the-less, situated where it is in a street of dated buildings, its originality still retains an extraordinary impact. And this, after all, is the important test of lasting quality in any building.

Opposite, stares down the other extreme—Sir Edwin Lutyens' building for Reuters and the Press Association, built shortly after the *Daily Express*. It is totally pompous—perhaps symbolising the solid reliability expected of its occupants. But it must be admitted that there is a certain grandeur about its entrance: a recessed portal capped by a vast circular niche and gilt figure of Fame. Down beside Reuters lies Salisbury Square, once the forecourt of the house of the Bishop of Salisbury. It is another Fleet Street backwater with which the twentieth century has not dealt too kindly. No. 2, for instance, must rank as one of the ugliest small buildings in London—a hideous 1930s construction of concrete with horizontal bands, plain glass windows and nothing else. The concrete has turned a streaky black and brown.

Next door to it, however, is a splendid survivor—an early eighteenth-century brick house of five large bays. The brick is brown, with red surrounds, and there is a fine hood over the doorway. In the far corner, Nos. 3–5 are excellent examples of late nineteenth-century Dutch revival. The red terracotta materials may not be currently fashionable, but the gables, windows and pilasters round the door are full of character and interest. There is even a sadly decrepit little courtyard tucked into the corner: a delightful aside, badly in need of better treatment. The remainder of the square is of less interest. The Church Missionary Society on the west side is a handsome, rather worthy, mid-Victorian building. And the back of the Lutyens' block has an entrance to a pub, surrounded by weird geometrical adornments.

Back in Fleet Street and over the road is Mersey House with the *Liverpool Echo*. It is an interesting exercise, repeated often in Fleet

Street, of trying to fit an exciting piece of architecture into a site only two Georgian bays wide. It achieves this by creating just a single bay with a large arch, topped by a bow window repeated upwards to the roof, where Liverpool's famous Liver Bird looks down over Fleet Street.

Almost next door is an even better contrast to the *Express* building than Reuters. It is the extraordinary *Daily Telegraph*. Where the *Express* was all for bold originality, the *Telegraph* went for modern variants on so many old-fashioned ideas that the block is smothered in confusion. Its style can best be described as bastard Egyptian, with its upper storeys stepped back like a squat pyramid, covered in weird motifs and modernistic fluting. Its massive proportions are rather like a large old woman, trying desperately to make herself up to look modern but failing miserably.

Beyond it things become even stranger. Nos. 143–4, the *Western Morning News*, is a fantastic Gothic creation. It is called Queen of Scots House and has a statue of the Queen in the centre of the façade. Down each side of the building run two pilasters done to look like lengths of rope. The Gothic is quite overpowering and must really be a joke. Next door come two good solid Georgian survivals—just to remind us what London buildings are all about—and beneath them runs Wine Office Court, leading to the famous 'Cheshire Cheese'. This warm, black-painted hostelry with seventeenth-century houses above needs no introduction.

The *Yorkshire Post*, still on the north side, is, as might be expected, a solid and noble classical pile—again achieving a certain grandeur with just a two-bay façade. The *Glasgow Herald* opposite is more imaginative with much marble and bronze and gold-painted details. Hoare's Bank beyond it begins the succession of Victorian commercial buildings that mark the end of newspaper-land and the start of more mixed development. Hoare's is restrained and boring Italianate style in brown stone.

On the north side, however, the fun continues, with the incredible modernistic building above the Kardomah Coffee House (strange blue patterns on the first-floor windows) and with a lavatorial maroon-tiled block for the papers blazoned in bands across each floor: the *Sunday Post*, *People's Friend*, *People's Journal* and *Dundee Courier*. In Gough Square, tucked away behind Fleet Street about here, is the fine eighteenth-century house in which Dr. Samuel Johnson once lived. It is now restored as a museum.

Farther on comes a welcome recess from the façades of Fleet Street at St. Dunstan-in-the-West. This is an unusual Gothic creation of 1831, particularly notable for its octagonal tower, which forms Fleet Street's most prominent westward feature: not quite a St. Paul's, but not bad all the same. And as it is approached from the east, the black spire of the Law Courts, and then the Courts themselves make a most exciting spectacle round it and beyond. Beside the church are two delightful earlier monuments: an Italian-style clock dating from 1671 with a renaissance sedicule behind it containing two men and some bells; and a fine statue of Queen Elizabeth over an arch, taken from the old Ludgate. In front of the church is a bust of one of journalism's greatest characters, Lord Northcliffe, looking remarkably determined.

Finally, on the north side beyond Chancery Lane, comes the magnificent Fleet Street branch of the Bank of England. Cleaned, its original resplendent white, grey and deep red, it looks every bit as stylish and opulent as might the Italian palazzo from which it clearly derives inspiration. Its red marble columns positively reek of wealth. The building is by Sir Arthur Blomfield. Whoever, viewing this building with Street's Law Courts beyond, could still maintain that Victorian architecture lacked originality and a sense of style?

On the south side, apart from a few late nineteenth-century banks, the chief architectural honours go neither to commerce nor to the Press, but to the law. Inner Temple Lane is heralded by a superb example of late-Tudor timber-framing over an old Elizabethan arch. The overhanging oriel windows, two bays of them, are brilliantly intricate and there is a distinctly nautical balustrade above them. It looks rather like the poop deck of an old wooden-wall.

Farther on and opposite Chancery Lane is a complete architectural contrast in Middle Temple Gateway, built just three-quarters of a century later. While the one represents the final flowering of the half-timber style, the other is the first flexing of muscles of the new classicism. Middle Temple Gateway was built in 1684 by a lawyer of the Inn and is as simple and handsome as could be. Four pilasters sit on a stone ground floor and are topped by a pediment. It might have been designed in an afternoon and yet it is one of the best pieces of true architecture in Fleet Street. Its calm good taste comes as a refreshing reassurance after the fantastic creations that have risen up farther east.

The Soane Museum, Lincoln's Inn Fields.

8-Lincoln's Inn Fields

Lincoln's Inn Fields must be one of the most under-visited places in London. The square lies hidden behind the multi-storey cliffs of High Holborn and Kingsway, virtually inaccessible to traffic but none-the-less filled with slowly circulating cars looking for parking places.

'The Fields' are very old, dating from early in the seventeenth century. For their preservation, London has to thank the lawyers —a profession which by accident of history has done so much to conserve the strip of London that runs north of the Thames through the Temple and Lincoln's and Gray's Inns. The actual decree protecting the Fields from development was signed by Oliver Cromwell.

Today its most prominent feature must be its trees—the quintessential 'London planes'. From the central piazza they rise magnificently, each one a contorted character of its own and lending an impression of great extent to the whole square. They frame the views of the buildings and draw the contrasting styles into a unity.

The south side has suffered the fate that has befallen so many London squares—six-to-eight storey buildings of no architectural distinction, erected in the last 100 years. The only possibly redeeming feature is the portico of the Royal College of Surgeons, designed by Dance, of Mansion House fame. But this is now no more than a motif on a façade that was disastrously enlarged by Barry in 1835. The College have completed their architectural degradation by demolishing the neighbouring Georgian houses, leaving only the charming Steak House on the corner. Down Portsmouth Street beside it, however, is that extraordinary survival, the Old Curiosity Shop—usually dwarfed by massive air-conditioned tourist coaches outside. Whether or not it is in fact the Charles Dickens original, it is certainly a delightfully quaint bit of seventeenth-century building. It is almost impossible to conceive, however, what the area south and east of it was like when this shop was built. For this area, stretching down to St. Clement's, was a notorious warren of tiny alleys and streets, home of every sort of vice. It was ruthlessly cleared in the late nineteenth century and the Law Courts and the London School of Economics stand ironically in its place.

The west side of Lincoln's Inn Fields, dominated though it is by the gloomy heights of Kingsway's backside, contains one of London's best architectural conversation pieces. Nos. 59–60 is the oldest house in the square (1640) and is by a follower of Inigo Jones—if not by the great man himself. In its day, this renaissance style of architecture was as revolutionary to London as the *Economist* building is today. Londoners would have gazed in awe at the classical proportions and motifs and wondered that anyone could have built such Italian—such foreign—architecture here in London. The house has stocky pilasters up two floors and fine pediments over the windows, including a fancy broken one over the window in the central bay. Across the top is a heavy balustrade, almost too heavy for the scale of the rest. The house has been stuccoed at a later date and would originally have been fronted with simple exposed brick.

To its left stands it echo, built nearly a century later by a man named Joynes as a clear tribute to the style of the Old Master next door. The comparison is fascinating. The Palladianism has become more refined and pure and, in many ways more Italian—a testament to Inigo Jones's essential Englishness. The proportioning is more slender, making the building higher and rather aloof. And it is faced in stone rather than the seventeenth century's brick. In many ways Joynes's building seems a handsomer one, and yet it also lacks the same character. It is remarkable how easily one can imagine the fastidious, immaculate Georgian gentleman stepping out of its front door, while out of the one next door would certainly be charging a rollicking Jacobean cavalier.

The north-west corner of the Fields contains an interesting piece of the twentieth-century reproduction architecture. Newcastle House, by Sir Edwin Lutyens, is a stylistic re-creation of the late seventeenth-century mansion that stood here—complete with steep roof, handsome windows and sweeping steps up to the front door.

On the north side of the Fields are a number of fine Georgian houses still surviving, and the scale is clearly as it should be—four or five storeys. But the most notable building is No. 14—the John Soane Museum. Soane was a lone genius in the late Georgian years—albeit a much patronised one—and this house he designed for himself in 1824 is unique. The façade, and the whole interior, are an architectural fantasy. It is as if Soane, in common with so many architects, had longed to break out of the restraints on his creative skill imposed by his clients and let his imagination run riot. Here it does. The front is an amazing conglomeration of motifs—Greek, Roman, Gothic, and, of course, Soanian. And inside is a sequence of spatial inventions and curiosities, full of hidden corners, hanging ceilings and sudden views. There is no other building like it in London.

Beyond it, towards the end of the north side, the twentieth century reasserts itself, with a vengeance. But ahead and to the east is a wonderful brick wall, with the trees of Lincoln's Inn itself peeping over the top. The sense of space this provides is just what is needed to prevent the square itself from becoming boxed in.

Chapel and Hall Lincoln's Inn

9-Inns of Court

If we were to take a map of London and put a star on all the most distinguished works of architecture, nine out of ten people would be amazed to find one of the densest constellations clustered along a strip running north from the river across Fleet Street and through Holborn. And they would be equally surprised to be told that along this strip lay row upon row of sumptuous chambers, spaciously laid out, with acres of private garden and with hardly a murmur of traffic to disturb their stately peace. For the Inns of Court have remained firmly hidden from the tide of east–west traffic surging along Fleet Street and Holborn, their tiny gateways forbidding the entry of more than private traffic and their conservative tradition resisting any temptations to development.

The Inns of Court were places where lawyers resided—and thoroughly enjoyed themselves—while practising farther west at the courts of Westminster. There were once many of them—situated in the vacated groves of the old order of the Knights Templar, who had built the famous Temple Church for themselves. But only four remain in their original function—Gray's and Lincoln's Inns and the Middle and Inner Temples. And their persistent wealth has put them, at least since the Restoration of 1660, in the forefront of architectural patronage.

Because of the richness of the architectural treasures they contained, the damage done to the Inns of Court by bombing during the war was especially tragic. But their innate conservatism, which survived even that traumatic experience, was sufficient to produce a wave of rebuilding which, although it was seldom imaginative, at least restored much of the area to its former scale and reproduced many of the buildings as exact copies of the originals. Would that other institutions had shown a similar humility towards the styles of their predecessors. As a result, the Inns of Court have almost no new buildings of any quality, and the Temples, in particular, have many that are utterly characterless. Yet they have succeeded in retaining precisely the scale and atmosphere which makes them so valuable to the London scene. And for this, at least, we must be thankful.

It is almost impossible to know where to begin looking at the Inns of Court, but it is probably easiest to start at the river, where the Inner Temple gives an unlikely breast of open garden to the sea of traffic along the Embankment. Middle Temple Lane leads through one of those buildings at which no one would have taken a second look when it was black and sooty. Today, a pristine white, it is a fantastic example of late-Victorian architectural self-confidence and abuse of tradition. There are round corner turrets, ornate stone balustrades and a luscious gabled roof. And the central arch throws everything to the stylistic winds, with caryatids, Gothic niches, cherubs, carved foliage, floral capitals—the lot.

But that is quite enough—and such flamboyance is not to be found anywhere else in the depths of the legal enclave. To the right, off Middle Temple Lane, is the area of the Inner Temple. The buildings in the first succession of courts were severely bombed and have been comprehensively rebuilt in a bland red brick neo-Georgian. It never excites but cannot be said to annoy, and it at least respects the cloistered courtyard principle on which all the Inns are based.

Pump Court still has original late seventeenth-century buildings in it—instantly recognisable from the 'neo' by the softness of the outlines and the age of the brick. Tanfield Court has been interestingly reconstructed, with cloisters at its western end, the new Hall to the south (with a bit of the ancient buttery thankfully surviving at its end) and the great Temple itself to the north. The church is the old home of the Knights Templar, long before lawyers were ever thought of in these parts. It is one of the few round churches in Britain, dating from the late twelfth century, but with an Early English nave of the thirteenth. It is much more impressive inside than outside—which has been heavily restored on many occasions. But the sets of three lancet windows and the soft brown stone make a restful contrast with all the rather harsh twentieth-century red brick.

Just beyond the church is an interesting exercise in reproduction —the Master's House. It is an excellent copy of the old one (1667) and shows how easy it is to re-create good architecture when there is the will to do so. And was the English large house ever more civilised in appearance than in those late seventeenth-century days?

Through to King's Bench Walk, the Inner Temple suddenly opens out in the dramatic way that all the Inns manage to do when they move from their Tudor to their Restorations and later sections. The north end of King's Bench Walk is a grand series of broad-fronted red brick houses, some attributed to Christopher Wren. They all have the heavy wooden eaves, the wooden window-frames flush with the brickwork (both a desperate fire risk) and the rudimentary renaissance door surrounds of the late seventeenth century. No. 5 has a particularly splendid set of Corinthian pilasters and pediment round its door—and still carved in red brick. All have old lamps on great sweeping supports over their entrances. Across the exit to Temple Avenue, Nos. 7 and 8 are still in brown and red brick, but are getting later. And the houses farther on are eighteenth century. Meanwhile, the great expanse of Middle Temple Gardens opens out to the right—making what must be the most lavish use of space within the confines of the City of London. In the distance is the invisible river—its chief usefulness being to lend an added sense of space to the gardens. But this is more than can be said for the overpowering neo-Tudor of Paper Buildings jutting out into them.

Back to Middle Temple Lane, and Middle Temple Hall is on the left just before Fountain Court. The Hall was badly damaged in the war but has been restored and remains one of the most precious Elizabethan buildings in London. Outside, it has the characteristic Tudor chunky scale with heavy buttresses. It is built of dark red brick with white stone dressings. Inside is a magnificent double hammerbeam roof.

Farther on are the united Brick and Essex Courts, with houses built after the Great Fire by the notorious Nicholas Barbon on the east side. This court, like King's Bench Walk, is badly spoiled by being used as a car-park. Through a passage on the west side is New Court, also with houses by Barbon, and with another of those leaps into space to the south over gardens to the river. By way of contrast, the far corner of New Court gives through an intimate gateway onto Devereux Court and out to Essex Street.

Fleet Street is reached, however, back in Middle Temple Lane through the splendid Middle Temple Gateway (see Fleet Street). The Lane at this end has some delightful late seventeenth-century houses with plastered overhanging upper storeys—almost like a seaside street.

Across Fleet Street, holding one's breath, and up Chancery Lane one finds the fine gatehouse of Lincoln's Inn—restored but dating right back to 1518, with square towers, stone arch and flamboyant coats-of-arms above. It leads through a maze of courts and passages which makes this Inn much the most architecturally exciting of the four—if only because it was the least damaged by bombing. But the Inn does its appearance no credit by filling its Old Buildings Court with hideous modern prefabs. This court is a priceless ancient relic of Tudor London. It perhaps looks too precious in its newly scrubbed soft red brick, but the fascinating octagonal corner turrets are there and the staircases each leading up to sets of rooms on the collegiate pattern—with no internal corridors.

On the north side is the chapel—early seventeenth-century Perpendicular Gothic in style and with a rare open undercroft in which lawyers used to do business. The vaulting in this undercroft is superb, full of rich Tudor details on the ribs, with roses, figures and shields. Its east side is enclosed by some horrid Victorian neo-Tudor by Sir George Gilbert Scott, who might have done better with Gothic. The comparison with the real Tudor across in Old Buildings is disastrous. Scott's scale in particular simply cannot match these tiny courts.

Beyond it, however, is a building on a much grander scale which can match almost anything. The Tudor perspective suddenly opens out to the length of Stone Buildings—late eighteenth-century Palladian and by Sir Robert Taylor. On the right of this lengthy cul-de-sac is a simple range in brick with only a central section in stone. The other side, however, is no more than the back of the West block. But it is faced entirely in stone and even has a porticoed section at the near end.

Back past the chapel and the scale is Tudor once more. Indeed, on the left it is even earlier. The Old Hall was built in the late fifteenth century and has intriguing bay windows at the ends of each wall. It is a friendly little building, reminder of days when Lincoln's Inn was, precisely, an Inn. So too is tiny Hale Court beyond. It has Tudor turret staircases—the one on the right being so big it has to have buttresses to hold it up.

Farther on is late seventeenth-century opulence with a vengeance. New Court is one of the most quietly handsome squares in London. It was built as a private speculation by one, Henry Serle, in the 1680s and then had nothing to do with Lincoln's Inn. But it is Lincoln's Inn which has preserved it, and which gives it an added grandeur by the gardens to the north. Here on the right, is the west front of Stone Buildings in all its late Palladian splendour. Rather than have a central pediment with columns, Taylor has given the façade two at either end, thrusting them forward to make their point more forcibly. They look particularly fine, seen, as usually they must be, at an acute angle from New Square.

Opposite is the equally impressive group of the New Hall and Library. They are by Philip Hardwick (the same, incredibly, as did the Italianate City Club in Old Broad Street) and are in a neo-Tudor style of 1843. Clearly the conservatism of the Inn authorities knew no bounds. Hardwick, however, did a noble job with diapered red brick and stone dressings, a Perpendicular Gothic window to the Hall and a suitably jumbled outline. Later additions included a rather unnecessary stone turret. Outside it and facing New Square is a set of gates of quite remarkable design—a convolution of splayed flowers and twirls of ironwork with which somone must have had great fun at the forge. And they appear to serve no purpose; there is no fence on either side.

Gray's Inn requires real ingenuity to find from here. One entrance is next door to Henekey's in High Holborn—the main one is from Gray's Inn Road. The Holborn entrance leads to South Square, and it becomes immediately apparent that Gray's Inn found its style back in the Restoration period, like all the others, and has found no good reason to change it. Buildings dating from the seventeenth to the twentieth centuries are juxtaposed in precisely the same style—right down to the doorways capped by broken curved pediments. It does not take much imagination to guess which are which, however. The patina of age and the dates above the doors give the game away.

Through in Field Court the buildings are of a later date, but the chief point of interest is the garden sweeping northwards. Leading to the gardens is a fine, restrained Georgian iron gate with a pair of posts capped by indeterminate mythical creatures, rampant. The gardens are superb, Georgian buildings to the right stretching away in exquisite perspective. They were laid out, so legend has it, by the Inn's most distinguished inmate, Francis Bacon—a theory lent at least some credence by their highly formal layout. In the distance, John Street extends the vista across Theobald's Road, turning it nicely to the left.

In the main body of the Inn and backing on to the gardens is the only real survivor of the seventeenth-century Gray's Inn—Gray's Inn Square. It is as magnificent an evocation of Restoration London as can be found standing anywhere. It suffered in the war but not too much, and has been well restored—three sides of consistent four-storey red brick buildings, almost all with the characteristic broken pediment over the doors. On the south side are the restored chapel and hall. The chapel to the left is early nineteenth century, with a simple pillared lantern on the roof. The hall to the right was Tudor and its external Perpendicular Gothic features and lantern are much more flamboyant.

But it is in the grass and small trees and unity of the whole that the period charm of Gray's Inn Square lies. And to go out through the handsome pedimented gateway into the roar of modern Gray's Inn Road is like stepping out of the proverbial history book.

The Strand

10-The Strand

The first thing to remember about the Strand is that it does not end, as most people imagine, at Waterloo Bridge, but extends right down to Temple Bar at the end of Fleet Street. It still is, as it always was, the great link between the ancient cities of London and Westminster. It still joins the world of work and the world of play. And despite the passing of the great houses that used to line its river side—hence the name, Strand—it still contains some fine buildings on or near its length.

Perhaps because of its historical role of being a suburb to two cities, the western portion of the street has totally failed to develop any real character. It is a rag-bag of good and bad hotels, good and bad restaurants, good and bad shops and a couple of theatres. And yet for some reason the Strand had always had a favoured place in the affection of Londoners. Approached from the west, it seems to sneak surreptitiously out of Trafalgar Square. It is, of course, centuries older than the Square, previously leading straight out of the top end of Whitehall. Now it is entered behind South Africa House through the maelstrom of traffic and pedestrians outside Charing Cross Station.

The Charing Cross Hotel is a decent Victorian building by E. M. Barry, architect of Covent Garden Opera House. Designed in a careful Italian style with an excellent use of different textures of stone, it was first harmed by the addition of two extra stories. But it has been absolutely desecrated by British Rail plastering a grotesquely unsuitable sign across the bottom in blaring modern lettering saying 'Charing Cross'—as if no one knew. British Rail's philistinism with its London buildings knows no bounds.

Opposite the station stand the beginnings of John Nash's uncompleted West Strand Improvements, intended once to stretch

Nash's 'Pepperpots' in the Strand.

right up to the British Museum. The Strand frontage is in a simple Nash classical style, stuccoed, but capped at either end by delightful round 'pepper-pots'. Up William IV Street can be glimpsed the corner of the Charing Cross Hospital. Designed by Decimus Burton it is emphasised beautifully with giant pillars, showing how flexibly the Regency architects could use classical styles on difficult sites. Here and round in Adelaide Street, at least a fleeting impression can be gained of the sort of town London might have become had Nash been given full rein. In the middle of Nash's Strand range, however, there is a sudden unfunny joke. It is Coutt's Bank, built in 1903. It is too grandiloquent for its surroundings and too tall—an architectural lesson in a nutshell.

Still on the same side of the road is the previous Rhodesia House by Charles Holden. It was built in 1907 for the British Medical Association at a time when British architecture was going through one of its most original periods—since when it has only recently recovered its form. It is solid and rather Scottish with a bold use of traditional motifs. The niches in the walls contain some early Epstein statues, scandalously mutilated by subsequent prudish owners of the block.

To the south, and down a side-street, lies the area known as the Adelphi. It was built as a dramatic speculation by the Adam brothers in the late eighteenth century—a time of dramatic speculations. Its conception was as original architecturally as it was commercially, but only a few of the magnificent Adam ranges still stand. In their place is massive twentieth-century vulgarity. The survivals are chiefly the Royal College of Arts in John Adam Street, a section of Adam Street and the west side of Robert Street. Further early Georgian individual town houses are farther down the hill towards Buckingham Street, all making a pleasantly isolated little neighbourhood.

Back on the Strand, however, is something of which this century can be more proud—Peter Robinson's store by Denys Lasdun. Although it dates from the architecturally arid fifties it is uncompromisingly modern. Concrete and glass are used confidently, but with a sense of proportion and, above all, the windows and entrances are not totally unwelcoming, as in so many modern shops.

The remainder of the Strand to Waterloo Bridge is steady dreariness—relieved only by asides such as the charming Vaudeville Theatre and the sumptuously ornate metal canopy over the entrance to the Savoy. Down behind it is the tiny Savoy Chapel. But the great compensation is the view ahead—the twin towers of St. Mary-le-Strand and St. Clement Danes sailing like ships down the Strand. It is surely one of the great views of London.

Past the crossing to Waterloo Bridge, the Aldwych buildings to the left were all built at the start of this century when the new Kingsway was being pushed through the slums of Holborn. They mostly reflect the brash ugliness of so much building at that time—for instance the massive imperial classical of Bush House and Australia House. The newer English Electric building on the corner, built in the 1950s, in place of the old Gaiety Theatre, is a good example of how little British architecture improved in half a century. Next door to it, however, is a none-too-bad *palazzo*, Marconi House by Norman Shaw, so much more thoughtful and stylish than his contemporaries round him in the Aldwych.

Across the road, however, the story is a very different one. A succession of wonderful survivals of Georgian and even earlier town houses flank the Strand frontage of Somerset House. This was British architecture in its golden age—the 1770s. And William Chambers's building is a perfect example of how well classical Palladianism fitted into the line of a London street. Everything seems right—the proportioning, the careful details, the superb renaissance loggia. And all is blessedly accorded due respect by the preservation of the original lower buildings either side.

Alas, farther along the same side rises the new and massive block for King's College. It is good in its way—stepped back to avoid too overwhelming a presence and original in its bold use of what appear to be plug-in concrete sections. But it is hopelessly aggressive, and for all its efforts to the contrary, totally crushes everything else in sight—especially poor St. Mary's opposite.

St. Mary's is a particularly lovely small church by Gibbs, architect of St. Martin-in-the-Fields. It is carefully renaissance, with pillars, pediments and apse, and yet totally English. Sitting there on its own island, it is, as Sir Nikolaus Pevsner says, rather like a casket one could hold in one's hands. Yet dirty and surrounded by swirling traffic, it looks terribly pathetic. Please, someone, clean it.

The Strand now wheels round to its climax—and climax it is. The view from Australia House down past St. Clement Danes towards the intimate warren of Fleet Street, with the Law Courts on the left, is pure London. No straight lines, many buildings in a dazzling variety of styles and just enough trees. The centrepiece is St. Clements, restored intact as the Royal Air Force church after gutting by bombs. It is a Wren church, using, as he so often did, the pre-Fire tower—although Gibbs added a few layers to the top. On its right stand two buildings splendidly representing their respective periods. No. 186 is a fine, noble Victorian *palazzo*, rising solidly out of the pavement. No. 190 across the street, belonging to Standard Telegraph, is an aluminium cube, cellular in pattern and imaginative in conception but horribly inhuman. It looks as if it lighted there by chance on a trip from another planet—or at least from the Barbican.

And down beyond them runs Essex Street, one of the very few streets still retaining its essentially late seventeenth-century character—chiefly because it ran into the grounds of the Temple and could never be a through-road. It was first developed by the great post-Fire speculative builder, Nicholas Barbon, and a surprising number of his houses survive in their characteristic red brick with stone bands. These were the seventeenth-century economic equivalent of the Knightsbridge luxury flat monsters of today. Some Victorian resident, however, was clearly having none of it at Nos. 36–9—a fantastic creation of arabesque decoration. Round the corner in Devereux Court is the marvellous old legal hostelry, the 'Devereux'.

To the left of St. Clement's stand the magnificent Law Courts, by the great G. E. Street. With the Houses of Parliament, they are one of the finest genuinely Victorian compositions in London. The succession of turrets and arches and colonnades, thrusting out into the street and then suddenly receding back, is superb, suggesting an almost baroque sense of space.

The Law Courts can be wandered round and gazed at endlessly —and frequently are by unfortunate litigants—always revealing new details and new moods. All that can be said is that if they were only cleaned a shimmering white, they would be appreciated far more than they are now. They should be one of the greatest sights of London.

The Law Courts, along with the tiny Jacobean entrance to Twinings opposite, the mock-Tudor 'George' and the magnificent lamp-standard on the island in the road, make an excellent signature to West London before the real 'City' begins at Temple Bar in Fleet Street.

Goodwin's Court, off St. Martin's Lane.

11-Covent Garden

Covent Garden is another of those extraordinary London amalgams. Just as Fleet Street is a mixture of the Press and the bar, so Covent Garden combines the glamour of the stage with, of all things, vegetables.

In Covent Garden itself the vegetables win hands down, making a colourful, refreshing and thoroughly Cockney side-show sandwiched between the smart office blocks of Kingsway and the bright lights of St. Martin's Lane. Essential to its character are the markets themselves. Their history is fascinating. They were originally established by the Duke of Bedford, a seventeenth-century developer who had had Inigo Jones's expensive piazza layout forced on him by the King and was therefore determined to get as much money out of the square itself as possible. So he established a market to provide revenue—a market which has flourished ever since, much to the annoyance of the early residents of the properties round it.

Apart from Jones's great church of St. Paul's, the piazza buildings have long since disappeared. They formed the first of the London squares, which, for all their Englishness, originated in Italy. And in true Italian style, Jones's buildings were complete with a grand colonnade over the pavements. Despite its obvious suitability to London's climate, this feature was rarely imitated, perhaps because in the early squares, each house was seen by its owner as an independent town palace and there was insufficient co-ordination to produce long colonnades. John Nash used a colonnade covering the pavement in Regent Street, but it was not replaced when his buildings there were destroyed. One of the few survivors is under the Ritz Hotel in Piccadilly—where it is a deliberate French imitation. Some idea of Jones's houses can be gained by the reproduction versions along the north side—not quite the same scale but the same idea. Compared with contemporary Jacobean houses they must indeed have seemed grand—as well as an extraordinarily bold innovation in pre-Great Fire London.

But if the creations of Inigo Jones have virtually disappeared, the market has lived on. The main buildings, and environmentally the most important ones, are in the centre of the square. They were put up in 1830 and might form the market of a small country town. They consist of just two storeys, with the sales area on the ground floor and offices above, all in a formal but friendly classical style, with tidy corner blocks, granite on the ground floor and stucco above. All round them throb and crash the great trucks of the wholesalers and distributors, with barrows and carts dodging in and out of them in murderous fashion. It is all bustling, crude, grossly inefficient and very human.

The market has inevitably expanded, spilling over into the streets round Covent Garden and taking over the houses of the wealthy (and the dissolute) who used to live in the area near the theatres. As in the Smithfield area, the penetration of a long-established market into a London neighbourhood has served to protect buildings and conserve an area that would never have remained intact without it. For despite extensive rebuilding in the nineteenth century, the surrounding streets still retain their original scale.

By way of contrast, however, it must be admitted that the tiny streets to the north of Long Acre, opposite Covent Garden Tube station, have no trace of that scale. Shelton Street and Shorts Gardens are quite fantastic relics of nineteenth century warehouse architecture. Suddenly one might be down near London docks—or even up in Liverpool. It is all massive, black, windowless walls rising above the roofs of huge trucks waiting to enter the market. How long, I wonder, can this survive?

Round on the east side of Covent Garden stands E. M. Barry's Floral Hall—all green and cream-painted ironwork surrounding lots of glass after the manner of the old Crystal Palace. It is a splendid illustration of the delight the Victorian architects found in working in iron and glass. Behind it is a remarkable contrast, the building of the Royal Opera House, Covent Garden—and designed by the same man, E. M. Barry. This time, however, we are back to the classical tradition with a no-nonsense portico and lofty stuccoed façade. Some of Barry's line has, however, been lost by the projection of the Crush Bar out against the pillars of the portico.

Opposite is the newly cleaned and outstandingly good Bow Street Police Station. It is in a surprisingly late-Victorian Palladian style, and with the turn into the alleyway beyond, makes this into a pleasantly Italian-style small piazza. Farther down Bow Street and into Wellington Street are some old-fashioned small Georgian houses—surviving doubtless by virtue of the vegetable market. And round into Tavistock Street are the offices of *Country Life* Magazine, an excellent example by Sir Edwin Lutyens of just how good his twentieth-century Queen Anne revival could be when used imaginatively.

The remaining market buildings are undistinguished, dating mostly from the end of the nineteenth century. Doubtless, however, the Victorian 'Wren revival' of those on the south side of the market would one day be regarded as precious.

Covent Garden's triumph, however, is St. Paul's Church, to the west of the market. It is unique in its stark, simple beauty. It is said that the Duke of Bedford, scrimping as ever, demanded of Jones 'something simple, like a barn'. Jones replied, 'You shall have the noblest barn in Europe', and proceeded to build just that. The frontage on to Covent Garden is extraordinary: a huge portico with massive overhanging eaves and four great Tuscan columns. Although burnt down in the late eighteenth century, it was accurately rebuilt, and today its immense power, lowering over the diminutive market and its smelly rubbish, is one of the most memorable architectural experiences in London. Behind it—or strictly speaking, in front—is a small garden and a sign proudly proclaiming it as the actors' church.

The streets to the west of the market once contained some of the finest old town houses in London. Almost all were replaced in the last century, if not earlier, but streets such as King Street, Bedford Street and Henrietta Street still have an atmosphere about them that is wonderfully evocative of the eighteenth century. In King Street are some remarkably fine buildings, including especially No. 27—the Westminster Fire Office with a marvellous thickly painted black ground floor in Regency style with grand doorways.

And down behind Moss Bros. can be found the sort of backwater that tourists always think of as the typical London, but which Londoners never know. Goodwin's Court, off Bedfordbury (which in turn is off New Row) is an alley of late eighteenth-century cottages in perfect condition, complete with bulging bow windows and gas-lamps on brackets. It is inaccessible, unknown and a prize example of what urban living should be all about.

Covent Garden is at present scheduled to suffer the fate of execution by comprehensive redevelopment. The market is to move out to Nine Elms in Vauxhall, taking with it 90 per cent of the area's character. And in its place are to come shops, offices, flats and hotel and convention centres—creating new congestion in the area which should dwarf that which exists already. However, the church, the area to the west, and the central market buildings themselves are protected in the present new scheme. And if the flats and shops element can be increased and the offices and convention centre element reduced, there is real hope of re-creating a new style which might not be all that different from its previous incarnation under Inigo Jones. The real test of this will be the use made of the market buildings. Here is the spot for a really urban bazaar—full of cafés, small shops, exhibitions, entertainments and cheap stalls of every kind. It could act as a shot of adrenalin when the fruit and vegetables have gone, and should be commercially viable as well.

12-South Bank

The River Thames never ran *through* London, as the Seine has always run *through* Paris. It ran along its southern boundary. And it did so largely because it was so wide. As the two cities of London and Westminster gradually developed over the land between them, the south bank remained neglected—apart from the little patch in Southwark round the far end of London Bridge. Indeed, London did not get a second bridge until Westminster Bridge was built in 1750. As a result, although the south side of London contains many delightful corners—and, farther out, many grand Victorian suburbs—it contains few streets or neighbourhoods which can compare with those found north of the river. And because of the lack of any real physical heart to the area—it has always tended to look north for its work and pleasure—its recent redevelopment has been harsh and unco-ordinated, culminating in the horrors of the modern Elephant and Castle.

It is worth pointing out, however, that many parts of Southwark and Lambeth do still have one important quality that is rapidly being lost north of the river: the scale of their older residential property and the spaciousness of many of their streets. With soaring property values to the north, many of the estates in, for instance, Kennington are returning to their Victorian status as desirable places to live within reach of the central city. Although they still lack the endless quiet squares and mews that were the stamp of the opulent nineteenth-century developments in West London, they have enough of the same character to experience a well-deserved regeneration.

They are, however, farther out than the South Bank itself—the name usually given to the stretch of river front between Waterloo and Westminster Bridges. And for all its architectural, and par-

The Hayward Gallery on the South bank.

ticularly planning, failures, it is so important an area of London that it demands some description.

The best thing about the South Bank is still, for better or for worse, the view of the north one. Once, long ago before the building of the Victoria Embankment, this would have been magnificent. Old paintings and prints show the buildings coming down to the water's edge while palaces and church spires pile up the skyline behind. Today the view is very different and is, indeed, a curiously unreal one. On a black day, the walk over the river at Westminster, along the South Bank and back across Waterloo Bridge gives an impression of a strange central-European city with a taste for unattractive monumental architecture and a lack of sensitivity in its details. Yet when the sun is out and leaves are on the trees the whole scene comes to life as the London everyone knows and loves. Perhaps it is that London is so usually seen in little bits and pieces from individual streets and squares that it is difficult to get used to it when seen in the round. London was never a Manhattan, nor was ever meant to be.

The South Bank—indeed all south London—is first heralded by the magnificent Coade Stone lion at the far end of Westminster Bridge, made from an artificial stone composition which used to be manufactured on this site. It is a marvellous lion, brilliantly resited from its previous home outside Waterloo station. The only sad thing about it is its off-white colour: outside Waterloo it used to be a true British red, which is what it should be.

To the left rises County Hall, home of the Greater London Council. All its features are, by classical standards, hopelessly out of proportion and its details seem the product of an extraordinarily uncouth imagination. And yet there is still something evocative about it. It could only have been designed—as it was—in those years of massive civic pride before the first world war, when London could say with justified assurance that it was the greatest metropolis in the world. From across the river even its pomposity can seem endearing, and as with so many mediocre buildings, the improvement that has come with cleaning has been immense.

An awe-inspiring aside to its lingering grandeur is down the members' entrance off Westminster Bridge—a huge man-made cavern of a courtyard steeped in exclusivity and aldermanic self-importance. Or is it straight out of one of Piranesi's prisons?

The riverside walk in front of County Hall is perhaps the

nearest London gets to a Mediterranean promenade. The only trouble is its distance from anywhere else. The lamp-standards are excellent—real street 'furniture'—with dolphins cavorting round their curvaceous bases. And set into the river wall are splendid bronze lions' heads holding mooring-rings. All that is inexcusably lacking are some benches looking across towards Westminster.

The view west from here is framed by the Millbank Tower in the distance, followed by the full magnificence of Barry and Pugin's Houses of Parliament—surely one of the greatest Victorian buildings in Britain. From here it combines stateliness with romance. Big Ben itself looks truly big—not dwarfed by tower blocks as it so often is when seen from other angles.

Across the way comes Norman Shaw's New Scotland Yard, looking like the bastion of security that it was when it housed the headquarters of the Metropolitan Police. Rising there, in red brick with rounded corner turrets, it must be one of the most powerful large buildings in London—yet it is at present not strong enough to resist the threat of demolition. Next door to it, is the sort of buildings its destroyers—the Ministry of Public Building and Works—created for the Air Ministry. What can one say?

But now comes the real surprise: Whitehall Court. Just a few years ago this was a grim, blackened fortress of a building, for which few could find many good words (except when they were seeing it across St. James's Park). Now, as if the wand of a detergent fairy godmother had touched it, it has been transformed into a shimmering white palace—all careful French château proportions and subtle motifs. And its gables and turrets, chimneys and pinnacles seem almost to float from on high across the river. Come back, you late-Victorian architects, all is forgiven.

Ahead the view is enclosed by Hungerford Railway Bridge, ugly and dirty but somehow rather quaint. If no one will pull it down, at least someone should give it a coat of paint.

The view to the south, however, is filled by London's greatest planning and architectural disaster this century, greater even than the destruction of Regent Street. For this was the most important site in London. It is the Shell Centre. Its featureless concrete façade and prison-like wings, surmounted by a glowering roof with house flags flying triumphantly, stands as a symbol of insensitive commercialism. It could not even be called a 'prestige' block; it has none of the searching after architectural excellence of the New York corporation skyscrapers. Not even a committee could have designed it (in fact it was Howard Robertson, who also created the ugly Post Office by St. Martin-in-the-Fields). As it is, the most vital site in London, left clear after the Festival of Britain in 1951, is all but ruined. Anything, even a skyscraper cluster, would have been better. A heavy responsibility now rests on the Greater London Council to make careful use of the site in front of it now occupied by a car-park.

Under Hungerford Bridge, however, there opens out a vista of real architectural brilliance. Ahead is the 'new' Waterloo Bridge, still looking extraordinarily modern although designed over a quarter of a century ago. And to the right stretches the Royal Festival Hall, the Queen Elizabeth Hall and the Hayward Gallery. This group is particularly meritorious because it was planned and commissioned by public authorities—subject to all manner of pressures—who have none-the-less been prepared to think ahead and experiment at each stage of its development. It is difficult nowadays to recall the aesthetic fury that the Royal Festival Hall evoked when it was opened in 1951. It was a tremendous leap forward architecturally and was the first 'modernist' public building in London. Now its familiar, rather dumpy, line has been drastically altered by a new front and by a maze of walkways leading to Queen Elizabeth Hall. Somehow it now seems less of an individual composition.

Instead the eye is led past along colonnades of mushroom-like pillars to the geometric jumble of shapes that is the Hayward Gallery. This building is to the seventies what the Festival Hall was to the fifties. It is bang up-to-date, and it is brilliant. It grows out of the South Bank and is attached limpet-like to the end of Waterloo Bridge. And its surfaces and spaces tease the eye so that they have to be looked at again and again. Each movement of light alters their appearance. While at one moment they can look cold, windswept and forbidding, at another the subtle textures of the concrete are warm and the scale human and inviting. The Hayward Gallery restores the South Bank's architectural credentials with a vengeance.

From up on Waterloo Bridge ahead, the real City opens out across the river. In the distance, rise the modern City skyscrapers: the triple towers of the Barbican flats, Britannic House and the blocks beyond Bishopsgate. But it is still Christopher Wren that holds sway over the skyline. St. Paul's rides high on Ludgate Hill, its dome conveying infinitely more splendour and presence than any of the surrounding blocks. And to its left, rising above the greenery of the Temple, is St. Bride's Fleet Street. Its famous wedding-cake steeple sends the Barbican tower behind it straight back to the bottom of the class.

Moored in front of them all, are those delightful nautical survivals—the *Discovery*, H.M.S. *President* and H.M.S. *Chrysanthemum*—satisfyingly pointing upstream rather than down.

Ahead, underlined by the parapet of the bridge, Somerset House is spread out like the great palace it is—despite the fact that it was always designed to accommodate civil servants, and still does. Its immensely long façade for once benefits from the shadows of grime that thrusts its columns and windows into deeper relief. Its roofline and thus its careful horizontal proportion have been lost to the Aldwych blocks behind, but the detail is still there—the architectural apotheosis of Palladian civility.

To the left of the bridge are a notorious succession of twentieth-century horrors—the Savoy, Shellmex House with its pompous pavilion, the new Adelphi and Charing Cross Hotel. On the skyline, however, can be detected the spire of St. Martin-in-the-Fields, and, to its left, the block of New Zealand House, completely dwarfing Nelson's Column just visible in front of it.

And then suddenly peeping out from beside the Adelphi block can be seen the one remaining jewel left in the battered crown. It is the end elevation of Robert Street, sole survivor of the Adam Brothers' river front to their Adelphi project. The pediment and white stuccoed pilasters show up clearly above the trees—a sudden note of grace and style, and making the whole view worth it.

13-Trafalgar Square

Trafalgar Square is the most important 'place' in London. Not only is it geographically in the centre, situated midway between the various areas of the city's activities, it is also the ideological heart, the old 'hub of empire' and the place where, on most Sundays of the year, the British manifest their fundamental political freedoms. The only sad thing about the Square is that its physical appearance so fails to live up to its ideals.

Prior to the nineteenth century, Whitehall merged into the Strand with only King Edward I's Charing Cross to mark the spot. To the north a shambles of buildings and streets led up to St. Martin-in-the-Fields. The idea for the Square, like so many good things in London, was John Nash's. He wanted also to build a magnificent route linking the Square with the British Museum, but he only got as far as the West Strand Improvements which still grace the Strand opposite Charing Cross station. None of the buildings in the present Square is by Nash and the result is a rather disappointing mediocrity.

It does offer one excellent view, however. This is the entry into it from Pall Mall East, with the portico of the old College of Physicians on the right, a view of St. Martin's ahead and the National Gallery frontage obliquely on the left. Gradually, as one walks forward, the full scale of the Square unfolds to the right.

It is the National Gallery itself that is in one sense the villain of the piece. Built by William Wilkins in 1838, it fails totally to make use of its location to provide an architectural climax to the Square. No section of its spread-out frontage really dominates the composition and it seems doomed to be overshadowed one day by higher buildings all round it. The strange central dome and little turrets at each end only make it fussy and diffuse. Walking along

The National Gallery and the Church of St. Martin-in-the-Fields. Trafalgar Square.

in front of the Gallery none-the-less remains a pleasure, especially now it is clean and white. And there are excellent statues in the grounds—one of George Washington and another of James II, reputedly by Grinling Gibbons. Perhaps if the National Gallery were set in more modest surroundings without a long view in front of it, it would be treated more kindly by its critics.

The area behind the National Gallery awaits redevelopment—and it had better be good. Orange Street, running along between it and Leicester Square, contains some charming smaller stuccoed buildings, as well as the back of Macmillan's imaginative new St. Vincent House—shapeless and cellular and generally friendly in appearance. But along at its eastern end is the occasionally threatened back of the National Portrait Gallery. Since cleaning, this building has really come into its own as an excellent example of the late Victorian Italian Renaissance style adapted to the wayward lines of a London street. It was built as late as 1890, when other buildings were going madly Dutch, or at least High Baroque, by the firm of Ewan Christian and Colling. The Orange Street façade, seen from the other end of the street, might easily be in Florence, with its splendid round-headed and ornate windows and heavy cornice.

Back in Trafalgar Square, St. Martin-in-the-Fields has been treated to similar disparaging criticism to the National Gallery. It is by far the oldest building in the Square, built in 1726 by James Gibbs, architect of St. Mary-le-Strand, and intended to fit the line of St. Martin's Lane, long before the Square was thought of. Its most distinctive feature is Gibbs's famous combination of Greek temple portico with a tower and steeple—a piece of stylistic bastardy that was widely imitated by eighteenth-century church-builders, especially in the United States. Somehow at St. Martin's the combination does not quite succeed. The tower, excellent in itself, seems to spring suddenly from the roof, subordinate to the portico. St. Martin's is a strange church, but it remains an influential classic of English eighteenth-century architecture. Note the famous 'Gibbs's Surrounds' to the side windows, with alternating large and small blocks of stone—much copied in the nineteenth century.

The remainder of the buildings are depressingly mediocre. South Africa House (1935) is a great white cliff and is plain boring —not surprising since it is by Sir Herbert Baker of Bank of

England notoriety. Canada House, on the opposite side of the Square, is little better. The original building on this site was a severely classical block by Sir Robert Smirke for the Royal College of Physicians (now brilliantly rehoused in Regent's Park). All that really survives of this is the straightforward Ionic portico in Pall Mall East. The scale of the rest has gone completely with later additions and rebuildings. And even the portico itself looks rather silly with so massive an attic towering above it.

But the real horrors guard the entrance to Northumberland Avenue. This cavern of a street was ploughed through the fine old Northumberland House in the 1880s to provide a mass of smart hotels. Now it is the repository of jaded offices and clubs and thousands of starlings and pigeons, enlivened only by the Sherlock Holmes pub towards the far end.

The only other building of note is the Admiralty Arch. Erected in 1911 by a grateful nation, and Sir Aston Webb, as a monument to Queen Victoria it makes a noble if pompous entrance into the Mall and on towards Buckingham Palace.

Which leaves only the Square itself. It was laid out by Sir Charles Barry in 1840 and it too lacks warmth and character. There is nothing of the Italian *piazza* or even the French *place* about it. The bollards, the steps, the balustrades, even Lutyens's fountains seem cold, grey and harsh in outline. Only the pigeons lend a touch of gaiety.

None-the-less, the Square does contain some fine things, which are all too often neglected. There are the two truly splendid triple lamp-standards on the south side, demonstrating Victorian iron-work at its florid best. There is the oldest object in the Square, the fine equestrian statue of Charles I by La Sueur (1675) at the head of Whitehall—the first of a line of such statues riding down towards Westminster. It stands on the original site of the Charing Cross and is the point from which all distances from London are measured.

And there is, of course, Nelson's Column itself. It was erected in a spirit of fervent patriotism in 1839, an excellently proportioned and justifiably revered symbol of British imperial pride. As to whether it looks better a rather indeterminate grey than it did before cleaning when jet black is questionable. But at least we are now able to see the Square as it has not been seen since early in the Victorian age. And when viewed through the columns of the National Gallery, with the terrace in front falling away to the fountains and then farther still towards Whitehall and Westminster, with the sun shining and leaves on the trees, it must be admitted it has its points. Which is perhaps why liking Trafalgar Square is no more than another way of saying one is English.

Holy Trinity Church in Euston Road.

Bloomsbury/ St. Marylebone

14-Euston Road

Euston Road is not for walking along. It was dedicated to the motor-car by the Abercrombie Plan for London a quarter of a century ago. And it has become one of the few London streets where buildings and scale can sustain more than three lanes of traffic. Indeed, despite its occasional flashes of intimacy, it is a street that can well be appreciated from the seat of a car—or even better from the top of a bus.

Euston Road begins on the borders of Nash-land at Great Portland Street. A last glimpse of less frantic days is given by the delightful stucco end of Albany Terrace on the left and by the graceful tower of Sir John Soane's Holy Trinity Church ahead. Soane never found churches particularly easy. He perhaps realised the problems of putting an English tower on top of a classical portico, and had more scruples about it than most of his contemporaries, who happily took their lead from Gibbs' St. Martin-in-the-Fields. Holy Trinity has a neat little set of four columns with the tower rising with characteristic Soanian verticality above them. Two simple round-headed windows hold the balance on either side. It is all a tidy, friendly composition and badly needed just here.

Opposite is the weird pre-war Great Portland Street underground station. Up ahead, however, are massed the modern blocks of Euston Road and away to the right rises the new G.P.O. tower. Suddenly, as one drives through the lights, the scale changes. Pavements cease to be places where people walk in front of houses and shops. They become windswept beaches alongside a swirling tide of traffic and beneath cliffs of buildings. Indeed, here they seem a total waste of space. The temptation is tremendous to accelerate to motorway speed and race into the Tottenham Court Road underpass.

On the left rises the new Euston Centre—suitably housing such activities as computing, data retrieval, colour television and the production of copying equipment. And beyond them stands the Euston Tower. It is a colossal skyscraper in brown and green glass—smooth, plutocratic and full of modernist vigour.

It does, however, provide an object-lesson in planning failure—a classic example of the effect of the Greater London Council's practice of only allowing high buildings to go up where the developer has proved strong enough to force them through. There was a powerful case, presumably, for keeping Euston Road low, running as it does between the late-Georgian areas of Bloomsbury, Regent's Park and Camden Town. And, indeed, the heights of most modern buildings along its length is comparatively slight. At some stage, however, the Council's nerve appears to have given way and heights began to creep up, leaving the previous blocks looking pathetically half-hearted. The best thing to do now would probably be to throw caution to the winds and shove up a whole cluster of towers here—and stop them going up at the same time in West London.

This nonsense is best exemplified at Euston Station farther on—with the planning authorities and British Rail as joint accomplices. The latter's destruction of the old station front and particularly of the famous Doric Arch on Euston Road can only be termed senseless vandalism. It arose from no over-riding commercial need. It was sacrificed to the god of 'modernisation' in the orgy of symbolic trendiness that seized British Rail in the early sixties. The inability to make use of old and valuable buildings in designing new ones is the greatest failing of modern architecture, and nowhere can it be seen better than at Euston.

The new station is well designed in a colour supplement sort of way. The line is low and clean and the use of materials is subtle. But there is far too much unjustified space, which adds loneliness rather than grandeur to the frontage. And it totally lacks the presence of its predecessor: it could never be called the Gateway to the North. In place of the old Arch is now a wretched little garden, surrounded by traffic—British Rail having changed their 'plans' for the site since the arch's demolition. The answer is quite simple. They should be forced to rebuild it conforming to Hardwick's original in every detail.

But the real madness of Euston is that the authorities would not allow the erection here of any tower at all—despite having permitted one just a hundred yards farther back. Not only does this deprive British Rail of much-needed revenue, it also makes Euston Square seem from the road to be a great big gap, losing all the scale and drama created by the Euston Centre to its west.

The Euston Road area has long been the home of organisations such as trade unions and charities—perhaps to enable them to be near the stations that can bring members from all over the country most easily. Their doubtless straitened circumstances have denied them the resources to do themselves proud architecturally. The neo-Georgian Friends' House, opposite Euston Station, for instance, is massively boring.

Farther on, however, the junction with Woburn Place makes an interesting aside from the previous scale of the Road. On the left is an early London County Council fire-station looking like a rambling country mansion. It is full of the Tudor and *art nouveau* motifs that were typical of the more imaginative Edwardian architects. The last thing one would expect to emerge from its interior is a racy new fire-engine.

Opposite is the grand parish church of St. Pancras, built in the full flush of late-Georgian prosperity. It was London's most expensive church and also the first to be designed in a purely Greek style—by the Inwoods, father and son. The son had just returned from Greece at the time—which is obvious. The main form of the church is good old St. Martin-in-the-Fields—a tower on a temple portico. But the tower is a variation on the Temple of the Winds and, weirdest of all, the north side has a bit of the Erechtheum tacked on to it, caryatids and all. The church, darkened by fumes even behind its refreshing wall of trees, is curiously pompous and cold—perhaps it is just that Athens in the Euston Road does not ring quite true. But it must be admitted that there can be few stranger sights in London than all those caryatids peering down at the traffic.

Their repose, however, is abruptly shattered as Euston Road finds itself again in more office development to the left and right, before opening out into one of the great vistas in London—St.

Pancras and King's Cross Stations. Almost everything the Victorians had to say is here; not just the personality of the two stations themselves, but, alas, also the commercial scruffiness of the shops opposite.

The stations of St. Pancras and King's Cross are the grandest survivors of the chain of great north London termini stretching from Paddington right round to Liverpool Street. They were built along the course of the New Road—as Euston Road was originally known—which had been constructed in the 1750s as a by-pass to the City from the west round the swiftly expanding suburbs between London and Westminster. It was the first known by-pass, certainly the first in London. The stations were only positioned here because the great rail magnates were unable to push them farther down through the Bloomsbury and Holborn estates nearer the heart of the city. Next to their stations they built magnificent hotels to rest their customers and celebrate their achievements.

St. Pancras Hotel was by far the grandest, and although it is no longer a hotel (though may become one again soon), it stands as one of the most important monuments of mid-Victorian architecture in Britain. Behind it, the station shed was one of the wonders of Victorian railway engineering, with its vast iron vault leaping an unprecedented span of space. In front of it, however, the company employed Sir George Gilbert Scott of Foreign Office fame. And although it is untrue that he used for St. Pancras the Gothic designs rejected by Palmerston for the Foreign Office, few people would guess that this building backs on to a railway.

Scott at St. Pancras used Victorian Gothic with all the confidence and skill that the eighteenth century before him used the classical styles of Palladio. The roofline is famous, with its turrets and chimneys decorated with frilly stone dressings. But less recognised is the way in which from the initial view of the towers over the main entrance porch, the full grandeur of its L-shaped façade opens out as it is approached from the west. Down to the left, facing on to Midland Road, is a huge, gabled 'east window'. The porch itself is in a free Italian Gothic style. And farther round by the entrance to the station itself, the ramp and balustrade makes an excellent perspective to the line of the longer façade. It is almost incredible that British Rail should have thought at one time of pulling it all down.

Beyond St. Pancras and subtly set obliquely on to Euston Road itself, is its sister, King's Cross. Was ever there more of a contrast? It was built some twenty years earlier by the engineer, Lewis Cubitt, younger brother of Thomas Cubitt, the great developer of Belgravia. Cubitt was no artist and was proud of it; there are no frills to King's Cross. It has a simplicity about it that is early rather than mid-Victorian. And there is no nonsense about pretending that this is anything other than a station. The two great vaults of the arrival and departure sheds are reflected as arches in the façade—built in a pleasant yellow brick. In the centre is a clock tower—rather the sort one might expect to find above the stables of a country house, but which has now come to seem an endearing touch on a highly functional façade. Down beside it is a respectable early-Victorian hotel, the Great Northern.

King's Cross and St. Pancras together represent the two finest architectural memorials in Britain to the great age of the railways. British Rail, successors to the ruthless but splendid magnates that built them, are utterly neglectful of the importance of preserving them and harp endlessly on the need to pull them down. As Ian Nairn has written (of King's Cross), they should no more think of doing so than should the Church consider demolishing St. Paul's.

Cumberland Terrace, Regent's Park.

15-Regent's Park

The first inkling of Regent's Park comes at the end of Portland Place. The severe colonnading of Park Crescent changes the architectural key gradually from the stone, brick and tarmac of a city street—albeit a most urbane one—into a vista of massed trees offset by sharp white stucco. Across the Marylebone Road and through Park Square, and the climax of John Nash's great triumphal route from Carlton House is reached—the Park he designed for his munificent patron, the Prince Regent.

It is difficult in these days of tight urban redevelopment, or minutely differentiated suburban estates, to imagine the scope of the opportunities that existed for the Regency architects—and particularly one such as Nash who enjoyed the patronage and the wealth of the Court to an extent that was probably more French than English. But there was little French about Nash's conception for the development of what had once been one of Henry VIII's many hunting forests. It was to become not a public park but the nearest Georgian equivalent to a garden-city: a lavish rural estate in which not one mansion but many would be cunningly concealed, giving each resident an illusion of it all being his own. Round it would be magnificent terraces, looking from a distance like grand individual palaces—the apotheosis of the traditional Georgian unified terrace architecture. And beyond it would be markets, barracks and small park 'villages' of detached and semi-detached villas.

It is incredible how much of this did in fact get built—and within the space of just a few years in the 1820s. And it is even more remarkable how much survives to this day. The Park itself, even setting aside the surrounding terraces, should rank as one of the finest naturalistic parks in Europe. It has an undulating rhythm to its contours, and an apparently ubiquitous lake which curls round over half the Inner Circle area. But the best part is Nash's landscaping, which was intended quite deliberately to give each of his palatial villas a sense of great individual space, uninterrupted by any suggestion that another villa was just round the corner. The centre of the area north of the lake is thus a great open sweep, while the trees cluster round the buildings situated along the Inner and Outer Circles. This hides them from view and gives an illusion of even greater spaciousness.

The area within the Inner Circle is strictly formal, and was once leased to the Royal Botanic Society. It is now mostly devoted to displays of flowers and includes the superb Queen Mary's Rose Garden. But it also embraces that least architectural of theatres, the Open Air Theatre.

On its outer circumference, facing the Park, can be found two of the four villas remaining intact from Nash's scheme (and only eight of those were finally built). St. John's Lodge, on the north side, belonging to London University, gives perhaps the best idea of what Nash was on about. It is set on an eminence overlooking the sweep of the Park northwards and is basically the work of Charles Barry in 1847 (though it was built in the original scheme by a man named John Raffield). Its fine stuccoed Italianate features look almost preposterously grand today. The Holme, also on the Inner Circle, can be seen from across the lake, down to whose edge runs its charming lawn.

The remainder of the Park, within the Outer Circle, is chiefly countryside. To the north lie the Zoological Gardens, containing much exciting architecture, but not strictly visible from the Park. They were first laid out by Decimus Burton back in 1827, but their most prominent external feature is the Mappin Terraces—man-made crags over which animals such as goats can roam freely and from which visitors can look down on the cages below. They were constructed in 1913 by a firm rejoicing in the name of Belcher & Joass.

To the west through the Park runs a decidedly French feature, the perfectly straight Broad Walk, lined with trees and offering splendid views to right and left over the gardens, the open park and the line of the Nash terraces.

The Outer Circle itself forms one of the most magnificent architectural experiences in London, if not in the whole of

Europe. It runs a stately course beneath grand palaces, past stunning architectural asides, with sudden rural vistas opening out into the park and cosy little gateways leading out into the big, bad city. And on its northern cross, it plunges into wonderfully dense greenery alongside the course of Nash's Grand Union Canal.

Progressing anti-clockwise round the Outer Circle, the terraces begin with St. Andrew's Terrace, with, at the end, St. Andrew's Place—a calm backwater with a Corinthian columned portico. It is marred only when seen from a distance by the wretched intrusion of the Euston Road Centre over its roof. Next to it, however, is the sort of brilliant diversion from the Nash routine to which no one could take exception—the Royal College of Physicians by Denys Lasdun & Partners. It is, first and foremost, perfectly in scale with the Nash buildings to its right and on the Outer Circle generally. The main façade is almost a classical parody: a substantial rectangle set like an architrave across two thin, upright columns positioned not at each end but in the centre. To the right is an utterly shapeless lecture hall in tough blue brick—one of the strangest building shapes in London, rising windowless from the ground like an architectural tumulus. But it serves as a wonderful foil to the stark simplicity of the white concrete of the main block. It all blends to produce one of the best modern buildings in London.

Beyond it comes a real intrusion—High Victorian Cambridge Gate. But it is followed by Cambridge Terrace, rather the Cinderella of the Nash terraces. It was doomed to demolition after being partially destroyed in the war. But after managing to keep itself up for twenty-five more years, it has finally been saved and will, indeed, be fully restored.

Now, however, the fun begins. Chester Terrace is massive, running to some 300 yards in length. It is hard to appreciate as a whole and must be judged too long even by Nash standards. But it takes the breath away all the same. The central façade is divided up into sections of varying bay widths as Nash tries to maintain its rhythm. Almost as if he knew he could not do it, he placed a huge projecting pavilion at each end by way of a balance. The pavilions are connected to the main façade by great triumphal arches, for which Nash seems to have had a particular affection, creating a tremendous sense of architectural drama.

Chester Terrace is followed by Cumberland Terrace—probably

the finest composition Nash ever built. It is one of the great sights of London, especially when seen on a clear winter's day from across the wild sweep of the Park. It must be admitted the other terraces look almost amateur in comparison. For once, Nash succeeded in matching his grand conception with skill in the detailed execution. The attics are none too overwhelming and the cornices none too ornate. The terrace comprises three main blocks joined together by recessed triumphal arches. The order on the columns changes from Chester's Corinthian to a more refined Ionic, and the roof is lined with statues in a Greek style. The central section, apart from having an unusual projecting order of columns, is crowned with a magnificent pediment containing a variety of figures in white on a vivid Wedgwood blue background. The pediment is pure ornament, having nothing behind it whatsoever—it is totally justified none-the-less.

Next comes another intrusion, a group in a late-Gothic Tudor style and in stone, not stucco. They were built in 1826 for St. Katharine's Hospital, which was moved from its ancient site by the Tower of London to make way for St. Katharine's Docks. The chapel front is a sort of mini-King's Cambridge, but the composition of the whole is suitably classical with the side-wings set at right-angles to the chapel. It shows an interesting flexibility of approach that such a development could have taken place while classical stucco was going up all round. The buildings are at present used by the Danish community in London.

Gloucester Gate beyond is back to Nash's Ionic order, with pediments this time on the end pavilions. The line of the terrace is spoiled somewhat by the enormous chimneys, which rather too forcefully make the point that this is not in fact a palace but a succession of *bourgeois* residences. Gloucester Gate gives a glimpse of the bridge over the canal and the road north to Camden Town. Down behind Gloucester Terrace and set on the banks of the canal, Nash set his Park Villages, East and West. East is a straightforward row of early-Victorian semi-detached houses. But Park Village West is a fascinating little close off Albany Street, with villas set amid trees in a variety of differing styles.

The north side of the Park was never built up by Nash and remained open. Today, as the road dives through the trees, there are glimpses of the modern versions of his nineteenth-century speculations. Prince Albert Road contains an impressive succession of blocks of flats, some of them of a high architectural quality, all of them lavishly opulent—and no wonder, with that view.

The terraces begin again at Hanover Gate—the Gate itself being a delightful little lodge through on Park Road behind. Hanover Terrace is sober and handsome, with three porticos complete with pediment reliefs and statues, and with a delightful arched arcade running the length of the ground floor. Then comes the most extraordinary terrace of all—Sussex Place. It is long (over 200 yards) and its length is relieved not as in Chester Terrace by occasional rows of columns but by polygonal turrets capped with bizarre domes—like something Nash might have run up in Leningrad. And instead of having pavilions at the ends, he projected sweeping wings culminating in double turrets and domes. Sussex Place, after lying derelict for decades, is now being completely restored.

After Clarence Terrace, believed to be by Decimus Burton and recently rebuilt, comes the specially inviting entrance to the Park from Baker Street. Ahead the magnificent Corinthian columns of Cornwall Terrace swing into view, with the west end elevation filled by a superb bow window supported by some tough-looking caryatids with arms folded. Cornwall Terrace derives a special impact by rising straight out of the street, its ranks of columns therefore usually being seen at a very narrow angle.

This is followed by Nash's set-piece at York Gate, with York Terrace extending on either side. The intention was to create an impression of two great palaces framing the view from the Park of St. Marylebone Parish Church to the south. If one can forget about the traffic streaming across this view, the result is reasonably successful. The church was designed by Hardwick, and is severely classical in form, with a portico surmounted by a tower based on a circle of classical pillars.

Beyond comes Ulster Terrace and the return to Park Square, completing a circuit of unsurpassed style and elegance.

Demolition in Woburn Square

16-Bedford Square

Georgian Bloomsbury is one of the great tragedies of London. Unlike the central areas of the city, it survived the great depredations of the Victorian and Edwardian developers. Most of it even survived the bombs of the last war. But what was once one of the finest examples of unified town development in Europe has since been destroyed by avaricious institutions and neglectful public authorities.

Just twenty years ago, it was possible, with a modicum of imagination, to stroll through the streets and squares of Bloomsbury and think yourself into a Georgian town. The street lengths, the scale of the terraces, the proportioning of the squares were perfect examples of their style—a style in itself as perfect a conception of urban living as can be found anywhere. Today, chiefly through the self-aggrandisement of London University, this is impossible. That no one told this institution either to stop growing or preferably to expand out in the suburbs is a lasting blot on Britain's regard for its true architectural heritage—a heritage of neighbourhoods rather than of particular buildings. And perhaps the saddest of all is that the last crucial link to the old chain of Bloomsbury's streets and squares, Woburn Square, has now been pulled down under a planning permit that, had it been requested today, would certainly have been refused by the authorities. They now know what Bloomsbury was worth, but it is largely too late.

Some intimations of the faded glory still remain, however, and they should not be neglected for their failure to make up an architectural whole. There are the pokey streets and shops in Museum Street providing a splendid foil to the sober majesty of the British Museum—a building whose massive black columns and extraordinarily unwelcoming staff seem determined to withstand all but the most intrepid scholars.

There is still atmosphere to be squeezed from the north side of Bloomsbury Square. The large white block on its north-west corner, housing the Pharmaceutical Society, is a fine *palazzo* redesigned by the young John Nash. And ahead stretches the simple Georgian terracing of Bedford Place forming one axis of the development going north to Russell Square. Sadly, the ground floors have all been painted maroon—a totally un-Georgian colour—but the style and proportion remain.

Russell Square was the largest of the eighteenth-century squares of London, and in many ways the plainest. This was perhaps why the Victorians, in a vivid illustration of how tastes can change, decided to surround the original windows with terracotta dressings. This nineteenth-century reaction against what was felt to be Georgian dullness seems today to be ugly and pointless—at least where it survives on the south side of the Square. The Square itself was laid out by the landscaper, Repton, with winding paths and odd bits of rock sticking up through the grass. More recently it has had lighting installed in its trees—against a fury of opposition.

Through the trees can be glimpsed the one survivor of the two magnificent and totally un-Georgian hotels that used to tower over its east side—the Russell. This building is almost indescribable—a fantastic red-brick and terracotta château, twisting north-European renaissance motifs into every conceivable variation. It was built in 1898 by someone with the superb name of C. Fitzroy Doll. It comes like a stiff double-Scotch amid the excruciating boredom of the other modern hotels in Southampton Row and Woburn Place.

Bloomsbury can again be recaptured farther north on the east side of Gordon Square with a magnificent terrace by the great Cubitt, matching his equally magnificent one in Tavistock Square. Both are in dark brick with white stucco on the pilasters and surrounds, creating an effect both grand and restrained. Cubitt also built the Endsleigh Street area to the north. And farther round, tucked away beyind St. Pancras Church, lies Cubitt's Woburn Walk. This is a small precinct of shops still with their late-Georgian fronts and complete with thick black paint, quaint balconies and ancient lamp-standards. They are unique in London, and fortunately protected by the local council.

Georgian Bloomsbury springs up again farther east on the far side of Mecklenburg Square, now into the estate of the Foundling

Hospital—and, many would say, out of Bloomsbury. This one remaining terrace is by the estate's architect in 1812, the young Joseph Kay. It was so liked by the governors that they paid him—according to Sir John Summerson—eight times what he had asked for it.

Farther south, the story is less happy. Much here has been destroyed by Rugby School, owners of the once delightful early Georgian streets round Great Ormond and Millman Streets. However, farther over in Great James Street, John Street and Doughty Street are some of the best preserved early-Georgian rows in London. Round to the west and into little Queen Square is an extraordinary plethora of hospitals, including the pleasantly Italian-style Italian Hospital.

But it is to one place and one place alone that all visitors to Bloomsbury should turn to see it still standing in perfection: Bedford Square. It was begun in 1775 by the Russells, Dukes of Bedford and owners of almost all Bloomsbury. The architect is believed to have been a man named Leverton, but that is not important. For Bedford Square was simply the complete and unified product of an architectural vernacular of the highest quality. Architects of that day seemed able to build magnificently almost with their eyes shut.

The general appearance of the square is typical of the Adam style of the period. Each side is designed as a whole, though with very small variations in individual houses presumably to the taste of the owners. The centre two houses on each side form a focus, stuccoed and with pilasters and a pediment. The remainder of the houses are plain, simple Georgian town houses—three main storeys and windows carefully proportioned from the pattern-books. Far too few of the windows, however, have their old paned glass left in them. Someone really should finance a restoration of the glazing bars to all of them. But the most notable feature of these houses is their doorways. They have wide arches surrounded by blocks of Coade stone, with a bearded head at the apex. Within the arch, the door is surmounted by an ornate fanlight.

The centre of the square is unusually leafy, and it needs a winter's day for the architectural unity of the buildings to be fully appreciated. The only intrusions on its Georgian charm are the Centre Point tower thrusting up over its south-western corner and the buses and trucks thundering through down Gower Street.

Bedford Square's great virtue is its wholeness. It possesses the quality which the remainder of Bloomsbury has lost: not so much the character of an individual building, but a general sense of unity and propriety. It is this that makes it one of the most important architectural monuments in London.

17-Portland Place

Portland Place was a lucky street. Built by the famous Adam brothers in the 1770s, it happened to stand in the way of John Nash's triumphal way from Carlton House Terrace to Regent's Park. And rather than ignore it or destroy it, as a modern architect would certainly do with a row just forty years old, Nash transformed it from two static rows of eighteenth-century houses into a dynamic sequence in his grand northward progression.

Little of this progression remains. Within the last fifty years, the philistines have destroyed Nash's Regent Street and Upper Regent Street. At Oxford Circus, indeed, his magic seems very far away. But the key to this whole section still remains—All Souls' Church, Langham Place. Its ring of free-standing columns, fronting a nave set obliquely to the line of Regent Street, and its simple conical spire, form one of London's best-known architectural features. It is now encircled by modern blocks behind, gripping it in a sort of architectural half-nelson. Yet it still manages the Herculean task of sweeping the eye round from the Regent Street axis to the Portland Place one as Nash always intended it to do. And the fact that most people do this sweep with no more than a double swerve in a car or bus makes it no less thrilling—though considerably more dangerous.

Apart from those disasters of siting, the B.B.C. extension and St. George's Hotel—All Souls' twin aggressors—the most important building here is the original B.B.C. block. It is a characteristic as any of the rash of hideous buildings that went up in the 1930s—shapeless, blank and dull with that nagging air of an age when people did not appreciate what beauty was all about. But like so many of those buildings—Peter Jones, in a different way—

Houses in Portland Place.

it is developing an antique charm about it, helped considerably by Eric Gill's statues and some weird friezes.

Opposite, however, sits the villain of the piece—the old Langham Hotel, now belonging to the B.B.C. This building replaced Foley House, an early eighteenth-century mansion whose width and right to a free view up to the fields of Marylebone dictated to Robert Adam the width of Portland Place. Its erection spelled the beginning of the destruction of this street. Incredibly, it was regarded when it was built in 1864 as daringly *avant garde*. It is in a jaded High Victorian Italianate style, known as *trecento*, and is one of those buildings over which no one should weep too many tears if it were decided to pull it down. If it is to stay, however, it should be thoroughly cleaned. For the Langham is a classic example of the thesis that it is often more important to clean bad buildings when they are on important sites than to clean good ones.

Portland Place still retains about it Nash's conception of a last fling of real town before the rural splendours of Regent's Park are reached. And we still have the Adams to thank for it. For despite the undistinguished twentieth-century blocks at either end, the scale of the original terraces is mercifully preserved just where it is most crucial, in the middle between Duchess and Weymouth Streets. These were designed not by the more prolific Robert Adam but by his brother James. The style is classic late eighteenth-century—brown brick (which now looks black) with distinctively lighter cement, a variety of railings on the verandas and arched doorways. Nowadays they usually have nineteenth-century stucco slapped over their ground floors as well. The quintessence of the James Adam style are Nos. 46–8, the only surviving of the central pedimented climaxes which he gave to each of the blocks divided by cross-streets. It is stuccoed all over, with a pediment and pilasters ornamenting the façade and two doors set into a recessed concave behind an arch, so as not to destroy the line of the front. The building is decorated by a very Adamish frieze and by some griffins rampant in plaques above the first floor. It is all immensely civilised.

The one regret is that most of the old Georgian window-panes have gone, to be replaced by gaping expanses of plate glass—cheaper, perhaps, but architecturally ruinous. (Georgian windows in perfection can, incidentally, be seen across Portland Place and up Chandos Street. In its north-east corner stands Chandos House, by Robert Adam, in pale stone with simple proportions and a handsome porch. It is one of the most quietly beautiful town houses in London. It also has a fascinating and exotic entrance to its stables behind in Duchess Street.)

Back in Portland Place, other bits of Adam crop up on the west side, as does the Chinese Legation at No. 49 in a later nineteenth-century style—and a very English one too. Opposite it stands, or rather rises, the extraordinary Royal Institute of British Architects. It is another relic of those terrible days in the 1930s. Despite its windows, which are a nod in the direction of the Georgian surroundings, the whole building is killing itself to be modern. Two pointless columns, topped by nude statues, flank the massive doors, and a huge central window with slanted sides leads the eye upwards Egyptian-fashion to where another statue is also looking to the sky. It is all a ghastly monument to the wrong turn that British architecture took in the inter-war years, when it should have been building on the strengths of its Edwardian innovators. Perhaps as a memento of that lesson it merits the historic building listing it has recently been accorded.

Nothing remains beyond it to divert the eye from the scene ahead. The massed greenery of Park Crescent and Square are a foretaste of the Park in the distance. And the columns of Nash's Crescent can be seen leading out from Portland Place, stately, stuccoed and full of movement. This, at least, is as Nash intended, and thankfully it is still with us.

18-Wigmore Street

Disraeli called Wigmore Street a 'large family of plain children—with Portland Place and Portman Square as respectable parents'. Today it is the way traffic avoids Oxford Street, in the mistaken belief that it is some sort of short cut. And no one could call it one of London's more significant streets architecturally.

None-the-less, it is a typical West End street which acts as the backbone of the Marylebone neighbourhood—one of the most civilised in London. This area was developed north of Oxford Street in the course of the eighteenth century round the ancient village of Marylebone. Indeed, the only crooked street in the area is the old lane that used to lead north to the village across the fields—Marylebone Lane. Today the whole neighbourhood is made nearly intolerable by being the nearest London gets to a New York one-way traffic grid.

The area was based on the two grand estates of Portman and Cavendish, represented by the two squares of these names at either end of Wigmore Street. Precious little remains of these squares—they were, alas, too near Oxford Street's grasping commercialism. Portman Square is by far the saddest, since it was still largely standing after the last war. Now it is all faceless modernity—except for Robert Adam's magnificent Courtauld Institute building in the north-west corner at Hume House. Cavendish Square, whose south side, like Portman, has succumbed to scale-wrecking office blocks, still has the twin Palladian houses in the middle of the north side dating from 1770. They are stone-fronted with columns and pediments and are remarkably grand for those days. On the recessed wall down the mews in between them is one of Epstein's finest public statues in London—the Madonna and Child. To be slightly retiring on the wall of what is

Georgian Shop-front, in Wigmore Street.

now a convent adds to its quiet magnificence. Georgian houses on the east side of the Square remain, and off the corner of the square down Henrietta Place is the delightful old brick church built for the Cavendish Square estate by James Gibbs, St. Peter's Vere Street.

Wigmore Street itself has changed its character with the changing character of its surroundings. As it was built up in the mid-eighteenth-century it developed as the shopping area for the grand streets that formed its hinterland to the north: Harley, Welbeck, Wimpole Streets and Manchester Square. They all drew their names from the various ramifications of the opulent dynasty that founded them. Most of the story can be told in the marriage of the heiress to the manor of Marylebone, Henrietta Cavendish Holles to Robert Harley, 2nd Earl of Oxford (hence Oxford Street) and in the marriage of their heiress, Margaret, to Bentinck, Duke of Portland. They had country estates at Wigmore and Wimpole. All these names live on as streets. Wigmore itself is a village in Herefordshire. (Nowadays streets are called after chairmen of planning committees, which is not all that different when one thinks about it.)

About the turn of the century, Wigmore Street clearly decided that its future no longer lay in being the 'shop around the corner' and its best bet would be to vie with Oxford Street for the big West End shopping trade. The gamble never really came off, and the chief survivor of the attempt, Debenham & Freebody, now makes a positive virtue of still being off the beaten track. 'Are you a she or a sheep?' it asks its women shoppers. Sheep, it implies, fight their way along Oxford Street. Since then, Wigmore Street has also reflected the altered functions of Harley and Welbeck Streets as the centres of the medical and dental professions, as well as the incursion of the modern office into the Marylebone area, especially at the Portman Square end. It toys with the idea of becoming a second Bond Street, with numerous high-class specialist shops, and even dabbles in the restaurant and coffee-bar business. And all in the space of a few hundred yards.

Architecturally, Wigmore street reflects this split personality. On a clear day, when the traffic is light, it can be seen to descend gently from either end to the 'valley' in the middle where the old Lane meanders across. And with this descent goes a descent in the level of the buildings.

The Portman Square end has been ruined by the erection of one of the most unsympathetic office blocks of any London street—the combined IBM/MMM building behind Selfridges. It is a building that Bond Street would never have tolerated. Up to the left, however, Manchester Street leads into Manchester Square, a remarkably preserved survival from the late eighteenth century but somewhat spoiled in appearance by the late-nineteenth-century façade of Manchester House, home of the Wallace Collection.

Back in Wigmore Street opposite, as the scale declines, is a lovely old Georgian shopfront near James Street. Its curved and paned window and fanlight over the door are delightful relics of the old Wigmore Street. Beyond it, at the corner of St. Christopher's Place, is the Pontefract Castle pub and a pleasant little Chelsea-style precinct down behind it.

As Marylebone Lane is crossed the style changes to that of the Edwardian period. On the left stretches the fantastic rooflines which that period produced—all gables and turrets and pink terracotta. There is the weird canopy over the entrance to that home of Sunday afternoon culture, the Wigmore Hall, and the Dutch front to the Wedgwood showrooms at No. 34. But the most fantastic building of all is Debenham's itself. For all its turn-of-the-century period flavour it is really hideous. It has great frilly arches, massive recessed columns, curved pediments and an ugly turret—all coated in inevitably dirty Doulton tiles. Will such a thing ever come back into fashion?

Wigmore Street ends with a flourish of cherubic musicians on the wall of a brick and stucco nineteenth-century house that turns the corner into Cavendish Square.

If Wigmore Street has never found a consistent character for itself it none-the-less represents a fascinating bulwark in protecting Marylebone. It is a front-line trench into which various Metropolitan activities have forced a salient from the south—smart shops, big shops, office blocks, chic restaurants—without ever having been able to penetrate farther into the heartlands of Marylebone. Its very characterlessness seems to have sapped their energy and weakened the developers' resolve. One day, Westminster's planners will come to put environmental management to work and seal off certain of the Marylebone streets to the north from through traffic. And then they can be thankful for Wigmore Street's good work.

Mayfair/St. James's

19-Curzon Street

Curzon Street is the epitome of old-style fashionable London—the spine of Mayfair at its most expensive and exclusive. Mayfair has had its architectural tragedies. The loss of the great houses was inevitable, but the loss of Georgian Park Lane, Grosvenor Square and Berkeley Square—all in the twentieth century—has been less excusable. They all became sought-after as offices before they became appreciated as architecture.

So, all things considered, it is remarkable that the streets round Curzon Street should still preserve as well as anywhere else in London the scale and atmosphere of the old seventeenth- and eighteenth-century city.

Curzon Street swings out of Berkeley Square down Fitzmaurice Place. This was once the site of Robert Adam's magnificent Lansdowne House, now overwhelmed by a hideous red brick block of the same name. The house itself has been partially reconstructed for the Lansdowne House Club in Fitzmaurice Place, though its surviving glories are chiefly interior ones.

Into Curzon Street itself and on the right stands the Department of Education and Science and on the left the Mirabelle Restaurant. Both serve the cause of excellence in their own ways—but certainly not in the field of architecture. The Department of Education and Science, like the Berkeley Square blocks, is the sort of stuff that should be demolished when Londoners become really civilised about their architectural environment.

The street then takes a curve and a dip past Shepherd Market, helped round its corner by the excellent positioning of a sedate antique shop sensitively decorated in dark grey and white stucco, just by the entrance to the market. From a visual point of view, this building is more important to Curzon Street than any other.

Crewe House, Curzon Street.

Opposite rises the Third Church of Christ Scientist—a massively pompous piece of twentieth-century baroque, and totally out of place in this context. But it gets away with it by sheer effrontery. Next to it is tucked Trumper's, the famous court hairdresser, by appointment to successive kings. And then come two delightful Georgian terrace houses, inhabited most suitably by a bookseller and a wine-dealer. The wonderful thing about Curzon Street is that such buildings come along just when they are needed to bring the line of the street back down to scale.

But it is Shepherd Market opposite that is the really priceless backwater. The low arch that leads from Curzon Street is still evocative of the slightly disreputable atmosphere of its not-so-distant past. It is on the site of the old May Fair that gave its name to the whole area, and was established by one, Edward Shepherd, in the eighteenth century. Although the stalls have long departed, the small alleyways, cafés and pubs give it an air of village intimacy which even the occasional office entrance or too-smart boutique cannot destroy.

Shepherd Market, Sir Nikolaus Pevsner has written, is a reminder not only of 'how carefully speculators in the eighteenth century considered the provision of shops, but also of the fact (specially important today) that the grand manner of Piccadilly and Park Lane is only skin-deep and that the more sympathetic atmosphere of the country town lies immediately behind it'. Shepherd Market could indeed be in a small English country town—provided we do not look too closely at its habitues. And provided also we can avoid the frequent views of the disastrous Hilton Hotel which lowers over it from the west and blocks out the evening sun from Shepherd Street. If ever there was a lesson in amenity to be learned, this is it.

On the other side of Curzon Street stands the only remaining detached Georgian house north of Piccadilly, Crewe House. Set back grandly behind a well-kept garden it has been mercifully preserved as offices by the company of Thomas Tillings. It is an early eighteenth-century Palladian house, built, once again, by Edward Shepherd, but with substantial alterations in 1813 which included the present restrained façade. It is all a wonderful survival from days when Mayfair was full of houses like this one, and everyone involved in its preservation deserves fullest congratulations.

Slightly west of Crewe House runs Chesterfield Street, in one of the few remaining streets in London that is still entirely composed of grand Georgian town houses—or more recent copies of them—as opposed to unified terraces. It demonstrates a lesson Paris has learned so well and London so badly: that in certain streets the character of the existing ancient houses demands absolute respect from later infilling and that it is even worth putting up unimaginative modern reproductions to preserve this character. No. 6 Chesterfield Street may be deadly dull, but who cares? It leaves the eye free to look at the rest.

Charles Street, at its top end, is similarly well-endowed. There are houses both grand and modest with railing, balconies and, at Nos. 40 and 41, some ornate lamp-brackets. Apart from the Georgian, there is also some good later infilling, making a varied but consistent whole. At the west end of Charles Street, opposite the splendidly rural Red Lion pub, stands a rare and remarkable weatherboarded Georgian house—painted a rather garish olive green. It leads round into Hays Mews and Chesterfield Hill, completing a neighbourhood of marvellous urban calm. All it needs is for someone to get rid of the tarmac and plant grass.

Back in Curzon Street stands the modern Curzon Cinema. It is not at all a bad building, looking well from along the street, although its massive ground floor inches up the scale more than it should. The villain of the piece, however, is the concrete, which is weathering badly.

Farther on, the houses on the south side become grander. There are some superb porches and doorways and at No. 29 some refreshing green creeper. Nos. 21–3 Curzon House is particularly magnificent, being seven bays wide with a grand Venetian window in the centre of the first floor. The whole row is as important a monument to the architecture of the mid-Georgian era as Queen Anne's Gate is to that of the days of Queen Anne.

Curzon Street ends, however, where it began—in the soullessness of bad twentieth-century styles. A little roundabout has been created at the top of the incline of old Park Lane down to Piccadilly and round it have risen some really bad examples of commercial hotel architecture: the Hilton, the Londonderry, and, slightly better, the Inn on the Park. All that can be said for them is that at least they are crowded in on one another—no money-wasting nonsense about wide open spaces here—which gives them a friendly intimacy. And at least for the moment they are all white, though what time will do to all that concrete we shall have to wait and see. Perhaps the saddest thing is that even the great Walter Gropius in his only substantial London building, and one of his last anywhere, could produce such an uninspired development as the Playboy Club farther up Park Lane.

It should all serve to remind us of the fate that Curzon Street has so miraculously escaped.

Burlington House, Piccadilly.

20-Piccadilly

Few people would champion Piccadilly as one of London's more architecturally exciting streets. It begins in the homely scruffiness of Piccadilly Circus—all people, traffic and commercial pop-art. And it ends in the arid wastes of Hyde Park Corner. In between it has no particularly memorable vista or skyline, and it has the unfortunate distinction of being one of the few streets in the West End where drivers can roar over the speed limit, freed suddenly from the jams of Knightsbridge.

But as with so many of London's main thoroughfares, a little burrowing can reveal much. Most of London's western streets formed, at some time in their history, the city's frontier on to the countryside. As previously in the Strand and later along Park Lane, the seventeenth- and eighteenth-century aristocracy built themselves large mansions with extensive grounds to enable them to live in their accustomed rural style, while still enjoying the social and political life of the capital. The very size of these mansions and estates doomed them to later destruction. They live on only in the names of the streets and office blocks that took their place.

The entrance to Piccadilly from the Circus was, of course, a part of John Nash's Regent Street creation. And, like it, it has since been replaced by an architectural grossness for which few can summon up much sympathy. The quadrant block connecting Piccadilly with Regent Street was constructed between 1910 and 1920 by that most boring of turn-of-the-century architects, Sir Reginald Blomfield (or does Sir Aston Webb of Buckingham Palace push him into second place?). Next to it rises Norman Shaw's Piccadilly Hotel, a great neo-classical monster sadly lacking the sensitivity which that great man put into his earlier buildings.

But it should get marks for its sheer bravado; its massive screen of columns above the main entrance certainly merits a cheer or two, as against a slow hand-clap for Blomfield.

Opposite stands Simpson's excellent inter-war building built in 1935 by Joseph Emberton. Designed at the same time as Peter Jones in Sloane Square, it proves just how good at least some British architecture was between the wars—and how sad it is that more architects at that time did not have the courage of the same convictions. It is remarkable how similar in basic form is Denys Lasdun's store for Peter Robinson's in the Strand, built in the late fifties when post-war architecture was beginning once again to achieve the quality it had already reached back in the thirties.

Beyond it comes that exquisite little aside from the commercial bustle of Piccadilly—St. James's Church. It was by far the most fashionable of the society churches and was built for Henry Jermyn as part of the original St. James's Square development back in the seventeenth century. St. James's has the distinction of being the only church by Christopher Wren in the West End, and it has many of his characteristic features—including warm red-brick walls with attractive stone dressings. Inside is much delicious Grinling Gibbons carving. To Wren it was his most successful expression of a large 'suburban' parish church.

St. James's offers not just the blessed sanctuary of a small garden but also the inducement to leave Piccadilly for a moment to explore Jermyn Street—named after the developer of this area—and the streets down to St. James's Square. Jermyn Street is most remarkable for its sheer continuity as village shopping street for the district. Like Shepherd Market in Mayfair, it still contains the type of stores it would have done when the area it served was residential rather than commercial.

Back in Piccadilly, and overlooking St. James's garden, stands a small branch of the Midland Bank. It is a quaint, amusing essay by the great early-twentieth-century architect Sir Edwin Lutyens, toying with his favourite Queen Anne motifs to produce a wholly original little building—a sort of stylistic cocktail.

On the other side of the street, up a small courtyard, stands Georgian Albany. This curiously English precinct began life as a grand house by William Chambers (of Somerset House fame) in 1770. But Henry Holland later added two wings out behind in which are now provided bachelor flats (or 'sets') of splendid privacy and opulence—but no longer confined to bachelors. Its past residents have included Byron, Macaulay and Gladstone. It is not possible to enter the path down the centre, leading through to Vigo Street, without being invited. But the character of the precinct can be seen from Savile Row behind (perhaps from in front of the Beatles' offices there, for those with a taste for the incongruous).

Farther along Piccadilly is the site of the estate of Lord Burlington, on which the first Earl built his mansion in the 1660s. But Burlington House's chief fame came with Colen Cambell's remodelling in 1715 in a pure Palladian style. Lord Burlington, his patron, was the central figure of the great classical revival and it would be true to say that this building was probably more crucial to the course of British architecture in the eighteenth and nineteenth centuries than any other in the country. It inspired by its example the wave of Palladian classical architecture which so effectively countered the development of the baroque and rococo styles that were sweeping the continent at the time.

Today, sadly, the quality of the original has been all but obscured by later additions—and in particular by the heavy Italianate block on the Piccadilly front of the courtyard, built when the house was turned over in the mid-nineteenth century to the numerous learned societies that now occupy it. But through the arch in this block (much in need of cleaning), the basis of the old house can still be detected. The top floor is a florid Victorian addition, including statues of artists set into niches: Lord Burlington would not have approved.

Next door comes the famous Burlington Arcade. Built in 1815, it is London's most famous shopping precinct. Despite its great commercial success in providing a peaceful and splendidly high-class atmosphere, its lesson has yet to be learned by traders in the neighbouring Old Bond Street, who still believe that traffic attracts rather than deters customers. Although essentially Georgian in scale and style, Burlington Arcade inexplicably received a new entrance front in 1911—an extraordinarily vulgar neo-baroque arch more suited to a pre-war picture-palace. It is great fun, though, and is the scene of many a daring smash-and-grab getaway from the jewellers within. Piccadilly Arcade on the other side of the street has never achieved the fame of Burlington.

But with its rather chic narrow bow windows, it is every bit as attractive.

Piccadilly has always been a street full of smaller shops than neighbouring Regent Street—perhaps because it did not suffer Regent Street's wholesale redevelopment in the twentieth century. Hatchards, the bookshop, is a typical survivor of Georgian days with fine miniature Ionic columns between its black-painted windows. Almost every main street in west London, it is worth recalling sadly, once consisted of row upon row of shops like this.

Beyond Hatchards stands Fortnum & Mason, London's most famous food store. It was founded in 1707 by William Fortnum, one of Queen Anne's footmen, but is now in a twentieth-century chocolate-box style, presumably intended to be reminiscent of its Queen Anne days. The ornate clock, supported on golden acanthus leaves, is its most distinctive feature—with a jolly chime.

Just beyond the top end of St. James's Street and the splendid sweep down to St. James's Palace is the Piccadilly branch of Barclays Bank. It is in a typically pompous neo-classical style with four fat columns on the first floor. But a tremendously exotic interior is visible through the windows—all black marble and gold paint. And the windows themselves are shielded by wonderfully luscious ironwork.

The blossoming greenery of Green Park is heralded on the left by that grand expression of Paris in London, the Ritz. It is a straight take-off of the Rue de Rivoli, complete with heavy, cumbersome arcade and even a Rivoli Bar. Over the trees of the park its roof might belong to some provincial château. Such a scene is deprived of some of its romance by the knowledge that this was the first major steel-framed building in London (built in 1906), though you would not know to look at it.

Green Park comes at just the right moment to prevent Piccadilly from becoming a bore. The road sweeps down and then up to Hyde Park Corner, following the picturesque contours of the smallest of London's central parks. It is full of hills and dales in which it is almost—but, alas, not quite—possible to lose one's sense of direction. The buildings are now, for the most part, modern and characterless. The new Devonshire House is a frightful substitute for the seventeenth- and then eighteenth-century palaces that preceded it. Nestling beyond it, however, is the Naval and Military Club—known as the 'In and Out' from the signs on the gates to its small front courtyard. With Burlington House, it is the last remaining of the eighteenth-century Piccadilly mansions, having been built for Lord Egremont. It was owned at one stage by Lord Palmerston. Opposite are some magnificent, but little noticed, Georgian gates into Green Park, relics of a previous Devonshire House. They are little noticed partly because they are never used, the authorities preferring to let people into the park through a scruffy hole in the fence nearby.

As the road rises towards Hyde Park Corner it passes more club buildings, their styles changing subtly from early to late nineteenth century as they move farther along. No. 105 is a fine early nineteenth-century house, as is No. 106, the St. James's Club. Their simple, carefully proportioned Palladian features, for all their modesty, look absolutely right against the slick inter-war modernity of the neighbouring Park Lane Hotel.

Piccadilly once ran continuously right up to Knightsbridge with narrow breaks only for Park Lane and Hamilton Place—breaks, incidentally, that used to get horribly congested right back to the eighteenth century. Now Apsley House stands marooned amid the swirling cars, surely the loneliest building in London (and known, incidentally, as No. 1 London). It was built in 1771 by the great Robert Adam. But the Duke of Wellington, to whom it later belonged and in whose memory it is now a museum, rebuilt the exterior in 1828—hence its rather severe classicism.

The screen beyond, by Decimus Burton, was originally intended to form a triumphal entrance into London from the west, fronting a great arch. The whole set-piece is now sadly awry. The screen and the arch, when built, formed an exit from the park leading towards Buckingham Palace. At the end of the nineteenth century, however, the arch—known as the Constitution Arch—was repositioned at the end of Constitution Hill. It is now at the end of nothing at all, but is stranded rather absurdly in the middle of the traffic roundabout. Beyond it, on the Knightsbridge side, St. George's Hospital, by William Wilkins, is a fine Georgian pile, if slightly dull. But it forms a suitably stuccoed foretaste of the splendours of Belgravia behind.

Hyde Park Corner was the London County Council's solution to London's most awesome traffic jam. As such it must be counted a success, considering the volume of traffic that intersects here. But how disastrous is all that windswept open space in the centre—

nothing but expansive lawns devoid of interest and thus of people and miles of useless subterranean passages leading nowhere in particular. Planners seem to think that grass makes up for road, when all it does here is emphasise the general bleakness. The best thing to do with the centre of this massive roundabout would probably have been to put a great funfair in the middle of it, or move Speakers' Corner here, or give away free stall sites for an antique market. Anything to humanise it and make the climax of Piccadilly into a real place.

21-St. James's Street

St. James's Street is a street of style and character, perhaps more so than any other street in the West End. Despite its massive load of one-way traffic, it still sweeps gracefully down from Piccadilly to St. James's Palace, filled with fine buildings and of just the right width to keep them in proportion—a grand relic of seventeenth-century spaciousness.

This area was once one of fashionable society and high living—springing up round St. James's Palace just as Belgravia did later round Buckingham Palace. But St. James's Street itself is now dominated architecturally by the clubs that characterised its eighteenth-century redevelopment. For if the clubs of Pall Mall may be the best known of clubland, those of St. James's are certainly the oldest. And while Pall Mall typifies the respectability—and often the pomposity—of the Victorian founder-members of its institutions, St. James's Street still manifests, at least architecturally, the stylish extravagance of eighteenth-century society—with admittedly frequent exceptions.

Tiny streets and alleys lead from St. James's Street itself towards Green Park. The park frontage was, understandably enough, the most prized quarter of St. James's. If the royal family could occupy the St. James's Park side, the aristocracy would monopolise Green Park. And they did so in no mean fashion. So jealously did they guard this strip of territory, however, that there is virtually no way through into the park down the length of St. James's Street. One alley, from St. James's Place, even has to burrow underground. Most of the remaining grand houses are obviously better seen from the park, but even from the St. James's Street side they still present a fascinating spectacle of sheer opulence.

St. James's Street starts at Piccadilly—despite the traffic flowing

Boodles, St. James's Street.

the other way it must *start* at Piccadilly—with a splendid view down to the Palace at the other end. The Tudor tower and gateway—built by Henry VIII, the real progenitor of St. James's fame—are set off slightly to the side of the line of the street. Over the top of them peeps the distant tower of the Vickers building on Millbank, making an interesting if not altogether satisfying contrast of old and new approaches to a similar constructional problem.

The west side of St. James's Street begins, suitably enough, with a club, the Devonshire, in the house built originally for Crockfords. It is a solid stone classical building with great Corinthian columns, but still slightly more lively in appearance than it would have been in Pall Mall. Down behind it is Arlington Street. No. 22, backing on to Green Park, was built by William Kent for Henry Pelham and has—apart from Kent's characteristically sumptuous interiors—a delightful front courtyard and massive porch. No car, surely, should ever occupy this precinct—it should be for horse-drawn carriages only.

Back in the main Street and cornering on to Park Place is the stately Henry Holland home of Brooks's Club. Built in 1788, it represents English town architecture at its best, handsome but always restrained. The front has giant pilasters with a pediment and frieze, the side has a fine Venetian window and all is in a gleaming white stone. Inside in its magnificent card-room, men such as Charles James Fox gambled away their fortunes, while in its basement, revolting displays of cock-fighting were held.

Brooks's was a Whig club, built in answer to the Tory White's across the road (nos. 37–8). White's today looks surprisingly more frivolous but that is because the Victorians tarted up its façade with sculpture. It was originally built in 1755, and the famous bow window still remains on the ground floor, from which members used to ogle at passing women.

A few doors down is the jewel of St. James's Street, Boodle's Club. Anyone looking at it would probably guess it was a Robert Adam house—that great Venetian window and lots of stucco adornment. But it was in fact built in 1765 by a little-known architect named John Crunden. The central pedimented section is offset by two wings with graceful white porches beneath them (compare Schomberg House in Pall Mall). The height of the wings as against the central pediment emphasises the architect's realisation that this was not a free-standing building, but was to fit into a street line (or is this giving him too much credit?).

Boodle's sits superbly well alongside St. James's Street's new-found claim to architectural distinction next door—the *Economist* building. This group, only recently completed by the comparatively inexperienced Peter and Alison Smithson, is a world-wide classic of what to do with this type of commercially viable development in this sort of area. Scale, materials, the use of space were all obviously the first, not the last, things to be thought about. Of the three blocks in the cluster, the one fronting on to St. James's Street is kept low and the proportioning of its windows is carefully Georgian—as is the use of Portland Stone. Behind is a raised piazza in which the blocks seem to sit happily, almost sculpturally, without ever leering over passing pedestrians. Much of this must be attributed to the gentle scale of the ground-floor entrances. They are quietly receding, not domineering, as at New Zealand House. And they help to give this group its most precious virtue—that it always seems to be smaller, not bigger, than it really is. Of how few modern London buildings can that be said?

Back across the road and down beside No. 63 is Blue Ball Yard. If one shuts one's eyes and opens them in front of the stables on the left, it could well be somewhere out in the country. How they have survived, Heaven and Westminster Council only know, but there they are as precious relics of the early nineteenth-century coaching days.

This side of St. James's Street now presents an intriguing, if not altogether happy, spectacle of the decline from eighteenth-century style to nineteenth-century brashness in club architecture. This ironically matched, of course, the steady improvement in the respectability of their membership. At Nos. 69-70, The Carlton Club—previously Arthur's—is still quietly Palladian in style, built in that great year for clubs, 1827. It is in a soft brown stone with good Corinthian columns on the first floor.

Farther down, however, things begin to slide. Beyond the suitably French-style balconies above Prunier's restaurant, comes the vacant building that used to house the Bath Club. The proportions here are generally grander, and the style of the details is more eclectic in its classicism, less detailed. But next door, at the Constitutional Club, the Victorians really let themselves go. The Renaissance basis all but disappears under an extraordinary weight of decorative foliage round the doorway and ground-floor windows.

Back on the east side, below the *Economist* building, is a massive exercise in inter-war monumentalism at St. James's House—which mercifully failed to catch on in this part of town. At No. 10, next door, the early Victorian classical scale is restored. And beyond we are thrown straight back to the early eighteenth century in shops of a type that must once have lined almost the whole of St. James's Street. Lock's at No. 6 must unquestionably be the world's most famous hat shop, tiny, dusty, utterly original and utterly charming. And beyond it stands Berry Bros. & Rudd, the wine merchants, in a creamy chocolate-box of a shop. It has a row of five windows with graceful Georgian fanlights above them and shutters that are painted a deliciously thick black. The whole building is lent added colour by the first-floor window-boxes. O for a modern architect who could create such a thoroughly inviting building!

Down between these two, and so easy to miss, is Pickering Place. This backwater, like a Parisian courtyard, is an almost incredible discovery here in the heart of the West End. It contains perfectly preserved small seventeenth- and eighteenth-century town houses round a cobbled yard. The last duel in London is supposed to have been fought there, secluded from the rounds of the police.

Outside, where St. James's Street turns into Pall Mall, the corner is surprisingly dominated by works of the late Victorian architect, Norman Shaw. On the south-east corner, Shaw used his Dutch style, with gables, red brick, friezes and foliage. Opposite, however, filling the end of the vista down Pall Mall, he was more suitably classical, using stone rather than brick, great arched windows on the ground floor and creating an appearance, from a distance, of an oversized suburban residence.

Down behind this part of St. James's Street is much hidden pleasure. St. James's Place and Cleveland Row are all one could ask as a place to live, secluded and with the park across the railings. There are many fine early- and mid-eighteenth-century town houses here—with some particularly delightful wooden-framed ones in Cleveland Row which might even be late-seventeenth century. But the real majesty is in the glimpses that can be gained from the end of this row of the succession of Bridgewater and Spencer Houses, backed up by the modern 26, St. James's Place.

Bridgewater House is by Sir Charles Barry, built in 1845, Spencer House is pure Palladian by John Vardy, built in 1756, and 26 St. James's Place is brilliant, restless modernity, built in 1959 by Denys Lasdun. The sequence needs no comment. It is one of the best architectural set-pieces in London. And it is what St. James's has always been about—elegant and stylish opulence.

22-Pall Mall

Pall Mall is a dramatic street. Cliffs of dark buildings rise on either side and the traffic roars down it like a torrent through a gorge. Cars, buses, trucks achieve a sudden release from the snarling jams of Trafalgar Square and hurtle down to disturb the eighteenth-century calm of St. James's and wake ancient clubmen from their post-prandial slumber.

The street's name (pronounced with an open 'a' as in bat) derives from the Italian *palla*, a ball, and *maglio*, a hammer, and refers to the royal game that used to be played down its length. Since the early nineteenth century, however, it has been renowned chiefly for being the heart of clubland—respectable clubland, that is. The 'social' clubs had developed rapidly in the eighteenth century, concentrated farther north in St. James's Street, many of them with distinctly raffish reputations. The Pall Mall clubs came later, many motivated by a desire on the part of officers in the Napoleonic wars to stick together when they were over. The fashion was set by the United Service Club, founded in 1817, although the Travellers—intended to mix men of many nations—was conceived even earlier by Lord Castlereagh.

Club architecture is a fascinating subject, since the Pall Mall clubs were developed at a time when the classical tradition was having its final fling but when Italianate styles were beginning to creep in. The clubs in those days were extravagant, wealthy institutions and the desire for grand and not necessarily utilitarian rooms meant their architects could give full play to their imagination.

Pall Mall begins, to the east, in Trafalgar Square. A row of exotic Victorian and Edwardian commercial buildings flanks the south side of Pall Mall East while Nash's charming Suffolk Street

The Reform Club at Pall Mall.

leads off to the north. Suffolk Street is one of the few corners of pure Nash domesticity in the West End—a broken row of stucco fronts with a portico on the right-hand side. On the corner to Pall Mall East is Reginald Blomfield's boring United University Club.

Pall Mall proper is unavoidably heralded by New Zealand House on the corner with the Haymarket. This early London tower block by Robert Matthew, Johnson-Marshall & Partners, was much praised and much criticised when it was built. Its virtues are that it is not, in fact, a tower block. It has little verticality and its strongest feature is the bold horizontal concrete bands emphasising each storey. As such it is a good 'London' building, blending remarkably well with its surroundings and acting as a stylish fulcrum on this crucial corner. Its chief vice is the old one of soullessness in its detail. The horizontal line is unrelieved and relentless and the great tubular steel columns on the ground floor thumb their nose at passing pedestrians. Stylish, perhaps, but they make a cold heartless corner to the Haymarket.

(The heartlessness can be relieved at this point, however, by the view back to Trafalgar Square. The National Gallery sits at a wonderful angle to the street, with its façade suddenly given new life and movement, and offsetting brilliantly the portico and tower of St. Martin-in-the-Fields ahead.)

Next to New Zealand House is the entrance to a delightful Nash curio, the Royal Opera Arcade, the first and surely one of the least appreciated arcades in London. It has a Parisian feel about it—modest and refined with stucco arches and large lamps suspended down the centre on brackets.

Opposite begins Waterloo Place, another of those architectural set-pieces which are the London equivalent of the French *place* or *rondpoint*—a space acting as a focal point for an area. The difference is that in London they are usually surprises. Waterloo Place has sadly lost much of its 'placeness' through being a mere traffic aside to Pall Mall. It has become an elongated parking-lot. But it still retains the proportions laid down by John Nash, its creator, and it opens out magnificently on to the Duke of York's steps and over St. James's Park to the towers of Whitehall beyond. In classic English style this conclusion to the sweep down Lower Regent Street is downbeat, almost too simple, rather than climatic.

The blocks on the north side of the Place are spiritless twentieth-century classical revivals, dating from a time when Nash's sense of scale was ruthlessly ignored. Facing each other across the centre, however, are the two epitomes of clubland classical, the United Service and the Athenaeum. The first, on the east side, is by Nash himself. It is a fine, noble building, but as so often with the Master's work, it was not his individual buildings that were his most successful. Its best feature is probably the two-tier portico on the Pall Mall side. The Waterloo Place façade, although splendidly restored, is a little too heavy and ponderous. The cornices and the involved surrounds to the ground floor windows are very much Victorian rather than Regency. And there is an intricate frieze against a green background just beneath the cornice.

It is all much more undisciplined than the stately Athenaeum—repository of old men of wisdom and letters. This is a brilliantly controlled classical building by Decimus Burton, although its original scale has been sadly marred by an 1899 attic storey. The noble porch, unusually composed of four sets of double columns, is surmounted not by a pediment but by a large gilt statue of Pallas Athene. A well-proportioned balcony runs round the first floor, supported on delicate brackets and with beautifully shaped railings. The frieze is a complete contrast to that of the United Services Club opposite. It portrays Athenians debating or otherwise going about their business in an orderly fashion.

The south end of Waterloo Place is still pure Nash. The Duke of York's column itself is by Benjamin Wyatt. It lacks the propriety of Nelson's and a little square balcony sits rather unhappily round its top, but its texture makes a perfect foil to all the stucco round it. And stucco there is in plenty on Carlton House Terrace. The old House itself no longer stands. Indeed, it experienced a relatively short life in the hands of Henry Holland and a few others until the Prince Regent's debts caught up with him and it was pulled down. In its place, Nash put the steps and the magnificent sweep of the Terrace.

Carlton House Terrace (see also Chapter 23) is one of those rhythmic successions of architectural climaxes that Nash so loved—in his buildings if not in his street plans. To walk along Carlton House Terrace, with its grand porches jutting out over massive 'areas', is to live well. This is the style of London—the gracefulness, the quiet backwaters, the soft lamp-light and the trees. And then, at the west end, there is suddenly a cul-de-sac, where one almost trespasses on the Foreign Secretary's front lawn, for Nos. 1 and 2 are his official residence.

By Carlton Gardens stands the new Wool House, aggressively modern in these sedate surroundings. But it has the right air of well-designed opulence about it, and the distinct three-storey block surmounting the entrance area breaks up its mass and helps it fit into the surrounding scale: not a bad blend at all, and its chipped stone facing should weather excellently. Beyond it, the backs of the Pall Mall clubs give on to secluded gardens, across which at night the ceilings of their grand rooms can be seen.

Back into Pall Mall, and the two clubs adjacent to the Athenaeum are the most interesting. The Travellers and the Reform both represented the 'new wave' architecture of the post-Nash generation of architects. Gone are the porticos and pilasters. In the case of the Reform—built in 1841—the stucco is gone too, replaced by biscuit-coloured stone. What came instead was the more modest style of the Italian palazzo, more suited to the narrow street frontage and less demanding of long perspectives and magnificent surroundings. Both the Travellers and the Reform have comparatively simple façades, with restrained doors and with immense care taken over the first-floor windows, which have pilasters each side and a pediment on top. Both these clubs were designed by the great mid-nineteenth-century architect Sir Charles Barry, before he turned his attention to the Houses of Parliament and the Gothic style. And their importance in the history of Victorian architecture can be seen in the frequency with which the palazzo style crops up in commercial buildings not just in the City of London but in city centres all over Britain—achieving its pre-eminence in the streets of central Manchester.

After an abortion of a building for Lloyds Bank—a sort of son-of-Shell-Centre—comes the massive Royal Automobile Club. Its classical scale is much too big for its site. One would need a clear view from the centre of St. James's Square to appreciate it fully. But then it was built in those terrible, architecturally ostentatious years just after 1900.

Beyond the R.A.C., however, stands one of the most charming buildings in London—Schomberg House. It is, incredibly, late seventeenth century, in red brick with extensive white dressings and projecting wings supported on ground-floor pillars. The central section is pedimented and a fine porch rests on two caryatids. It was built for a Dutchman, the Duke of Schomberg, and in its day must have been very grand indeed. Today, it seems friendly and jolly among all the sombre buildings of Pall Mall. Its left wing is in fact a twentieth-century reconstruction—but who's to know?

A few doors farther down, the club classical returns with a vengeance at the Oxford and Cambridge Club by Smirke. It has a fine great doorway and a stuccoed façade, enlivened by the colourful crests of the two ancient universities and by reliefs above the first-floor windows.

The north side of Pall Mall is a great disappointment. The old Junior Carlton Club has gone, as has the Army and Navy—to be replaced by mediocre 1960s versions of Pall Mall club architecture.

The only remaining delight is the ushering out of Pall Mall into St. James's Palace—surely the most restrained, domestic palace in the world. It rambles round, never showing off but never losing its poise until Lancaster House looms up ahead. This little corner of Royal London is a perfect spot in which to regain one's sense of domestic proportion after the sombre splendour of the clubs of Pall Mall.

Westminster

23-St. James's Park

St. James's Park was the monarchy's finest gift to London. Its area, to the west of the Mall, was preserved from development for centuries, first as a private royal park and then as a public one. Today it is not only a precious lung for the office-workers of Whitehall and Westminster, it is also one of the finest 'landscaped' ornamental parks in any European city. As the great French garden designer, Le Notre, replied to Charles II who had asked him to redesign it, he 'was of the opinion that the natural simplicity of this Park, its rural and in some places wild character, had something more grand than he could impart to it'.

The Park as it is today is the handiwork of successive monarchs —Henry VIII, James I, Charles II, and finally the Prince Regent with the aid of the ubiquitous John Nash.

St. James's Park is one of the smallest London parks, and yet it can digest hundreds of people—mostly Civil Servants at lunchtime—and still seem spacious. This greatest of virtues is achieved by means of extensive paths diving in and out of trees and by the brilliant positioning of trees round the lake. Each few yards produces a new view and a new sense of space.

The lake itself is a work of art, the art again of John Nash, who created it out of what was previously a long straight ornamental canal. So cunningly is it laid out that, to the casual stroller, it appears like a succession of separate lakes. Across it used to spring a small suspension bridge—recently demolished and replaced by a white concrete one. It must be admitted, however, that the new is every bit as distinguished as the old—a salutary example for arch-preservationists. Its immensely delicate span seems to glide horizontally across the water, restrained but unashamed. On

Whitehall and Horse Guard's Parade from St. James's Park.

occasions when there is a slight mist on the water, it seems as if walkers on the bridge are moving on air.

But the real joy of this bridge is of the views that can be had from it in both directions. To the west, Buckingham Palace's façade appears framed by massed foliage, like a country house seen from a distant part of the estate. It is best seen in the evening with the sun setting behind it, glinting through the trees. The priceless view, however, is to the east across the Horse Guards to Whitehall and Whitehall Court. Here the towers and roof-tops and turrets soar above the trees, creating, especially when floodlit at dusk, a quite breathtaking sensation of an enchanted city. Anywhere else in Europe this view would have been 'sorted out'. Roofs would have been realigned, vistas arranged symmetrically and a sense of order imposed on it all. In St. James's Park, as Le Notre so imaginatively realised, such efforts would have been disastrous. The beauty is in the jumble of shapes and perspectives. And let no one tamper with it.

The Park is bounded to the north by the Mall. It is one of London's few processional streets, a sort of mini-Champs-Elysées from the Admiralty Arch to Buckingham Palace. It was laid out by Sir Aston Webb as a national monument to Queen Victoria after her death, complete with Triumphal Arch, red tarmac, an extraordinary wedding-cake statue in front of Buckingham Palace and a whole new façade on the Palace itself. The new façade is utterly undistinguished, especially when compared with the gentle Regency one it replaced. But the Mall itself is undoubtedly a fine piece of work. It is now restored to its old role of a promenade when, on Sundays, traffic is excluded from its length.

On its right runs a succession of Royal palaces and great houses. First of all, Lancaster and Clarence Houses turn the corner to Green Park. They were built in 1825, the first by Benjamin Wyatt, the second by John Nash, as grand residences for members of the Royal Family. Both are far more sumptuous inside than their rather austerely English exteriors. Clarence House is now the home of the Queen Mother, while Lancaster House, much altered, is used for official state functions.

Next, St. James's Palace (see Pall Mall) looks most unpalatial, almost a friendly Tudor hostelry, with no real centrepiece but with a succession of charming courtyards. Although still the official home of the Court and containing a number of offices of the Royal household, it always seems something of a historic backwater. And so much the better.

Marlborough House was built by Sir Christopher Wren in 1710 and has his typical Queen Anne red brick and white dressings. Next to it is Inigo Jones's much earlier Queen's Chapel—the first classical church in Britain (1626)—exquisitely designed and much neglected.

But certainly the Mall's most impressive feature is John Nash's Carlton House Terrace—not a palace but supplanting the Prince Regent's short-lived Carlton House where now the Duke of York's Column rises. The Mall frontage of the Terrace is magnificent—rivalling the same architect's Regent's Park terraces. Its lofty rows of columns, its immense and ornate pediments and its huge sweep of white stucco typifies the stylish brashness of the Regency period. And the dumpy iron colonnade of the lower terrace on the Mall makes a noble podium for the main terrace above. The whole terrace is in the process of being cleaned and restored, an outrageously expensive job partly because they have been decaying for so long and partly because Nash built them so shoddily.

Across the Mall, however, the scene becomes once more confused and English. It begins with the extraordinary Citadel, a world war two bomb-proof fortress now overgrown with creeper and with a camouflage lawn on top. It is an impressive reminder of how little military building style had changed between the middle ages and the 1940s—but how much it would need to change to resist modern weapons today.

Next comes the Horse Guards Parade. It was designed by the great Palladian architect, William Kent, and is the scene of the annual Trooping the Colour ceremony—and little else. The long, low range of buildings is an excellent example of the restraint of English eighteenth-century architecture. There are few traces of baroque excitement; all is simple and well proportioned. Yet this was built by the War Ministry of one of the world's greatest military powers! With equally admirable restraint, the authorities have resisted the temptation of making the parade ground into a car-park—except occasionally in emergencies. For most of the year, it is a splendid sweep of pure, sandy space.

Beyond it stands Downing Street (see Whitehall), with the gardens of the official residences of the Prime Minister, Chancellor of the Exchequer and Government Chief Whip sprouting over the top of a suitably forbidding brick wall.

On the other side of Downing Street stands the Foreign Office. Built in the mid-nineteenth century, after a great competition, by Sir Gilbert Scott, it is in an Italian renaissance style, intended to express the Victorian spirit of solid imperial grandeur. It is in extraordinary contrast to the same architect's Gothic St. Pancras Station built soon after. It is a fine building and one day it will doubtless be regarded as a great one. But today Scott's lavish multi-coloured stonework and his intricate medallions are barely discernible under a thick coating of grime.

Beyond the Foreign Office are more government offices in a grand classical style, much less exciting than the Foreign Office and probably doomed to demolition. Along the west side of the Park runs Birdcage Walk—named after a part of James I's royal menagerie. At its Buckingham Palace end are the Wellington Barracks in fine late-Georgian stucco. They now have a good modern chapel replacing the one destroyed in the war, but it is unfortunately dwarfed by the hideous office blocks of Petty France behind it.

The real jewel of this area, however, is behind and backing on to Birdcage Walk: Queen Anne's Gate. The street is in two halves, with the oldest and best to the west where a wall used to divide it into an L-shaped close. It was built at the start of the eighteenth century and is the best surviving example of the Queen Anne style of town architecture in London. Like similar houses in Cheyne Walk, Chelsea, they are much larger and grander than later Georgian ones and are still reminiscent of the detached country house. Different coloured brick, stone and paint were still used to give depth and contrast to the exterior. White bands separate each floor and little stone devils surmount each window. But their most distinctive feature is their porches—splendid ornate canopies harking back to florid seventeenth-century plaster-work, with freely designed brackets and grand steps and railings.

Half-way along Queen Anne's Gate is a statue of the Queen herself set into the wall. Beyond it, the houses are later, about 1780, their smallness and plainer features illustrating perfectly the course of London domestic architecture in the eighteenth century. But they do still have charming old lamp-brackets outside their doors. Round the corner in Old Queen Street are more

Georgian houses—with some fairly discreet nineteenth- and twentieth-century infilling. Cockpit Steps lead down and back into St. James's Park.

24 - Whitehall

Whitehall is the most important street in London—and in more senses than the purely architectural. Throughout its history, it has symbolised the separation of powers between Parliament and the executive. Whitehall Palace, which gave it its name, was built in the sixteenth century by the resplendent Henry VIII, and it remained the Westminster home of the monarchy right through the Tudor and Stuart dynasties until William III built himself Kensington Palace. In 1698, however, it was burned to the ground, leaving only the stone gates and Inigo Jones's great Italian Banqueting Hall still standing. But although the monarchy departed, the great departments of state remained to be redeveloped piecemeal along the course of the street called Whitehall in the two centuries that followed. The result is the most dramatic compendium in London of the styles that have dominated British secular achitecture over the past two and a half centuries. Whitehall is London's most prized 'architectural museum' street—yet it is a street that is shabbily treated and most vulnerable to destructive redevelopment, either in spite of or because of the fact that it is almost entirely owned by the government.

But let's start at the beginning. The first crucial feature of Whitehall is its shape—that casual English curve which is so characteristic of every street formed before classical concepts of town planning arrived on the scene. It adds a touch of the High Street to Whitehall's triumphal progress. At its northernmost end, where once it joined the Strand at Charing Cross, Whitehall now pours out of Trafalgar Square like a river suddenly running through a gorge. Smaller buildings crowd it in on every side, giving an impression, after the grand spaces of the Square, of an intimate, almost domestic, street. It is an impression of human

The Banqueting House in Whitehall.

scale that appears to wane as the grand public architecture is reached later on, but which is subtly reasserted at the far end in Parliament Street. And it is an impression which is so vitally important to the character of the street as a whole.

On the right stands the traditional home of London farce, the Whitehall Theatre—so improbably, even ironically, situated here in this immensely serious corner of the West End. Opposite are simple eighteenth-century buildings containing shops and cafeterias. Blocks such as this could presumably earn someone a fortune if they were developed—but thank goodness they have not been so far. What would tens of thousands of clerical workers do at lunchtime if they were?

Tucked down behind them, however, is a fascinating relic of a former and more spacious age. In Craig's Court stands the façade of the old Harrington House, incongruously incorporated into the much wider block of a new telephone exchange. Harrington House was once a detached mansion built in the early years of the eighteenth century. It is of red brick, with a fine pedimented central section and a noble Georgian doorway added some years later.

Back in Whitehall, the street begins to broaden out into its full magnificence. From here can be seen the line of fine equestrian statues that ride down its length towards Parliament Square, like ships sailing down the centre of a wide river. On the right comes the first of the government buildings, the Admiralty. It is in itself an uninspiring building designed by one of its own Civil Servants in 1722. It is in red brick with four huge columns supporting a pediment across its entrance. The whole thing is lifted to architectural brilliance, however, by the screen running along the Whitehall front. This is a delightful early work by Robert Adam and shows all his characteristic lightness of touch. It is a deftly articulated sequence of pediment, columns and arch, decorated by two sea-horses and other suitably nautical motifs. And it throws the tall Admiralty columns behind into perfect relief—just as a good screen should.

Next to it comes Admiralty House, a simple late-Georgian building by S. P. Cockerell with a handsome Venetian window in the centre. And beyond it stands the Paymaster General's Office, a classic eighteenth-century town house let straight on to the street. Its soft pink brick and unostentatious details suggest a building in a small country town rather than the home of a department of state.

Then comes the Horse Guards—as much abused by architectural historians as it is loved by the tourists. Certainly the balance struck by the architect, William Kent, between the various sections of the composition—in particular between the wings and the central pedimented section—seems sadly out of true; it is vaguely reminiscent of the rushed-together stables of some large country house. But the proportioning of the individual blocks in simple Palladian style, and the modest, warm stone, play a vital part in maintaining the downbeat charm of this part of Whitehall. And the good old-fashioned smell of horses makes all the difference.

Where the Horse Guards buildings are rough and restless, Dover House, next door, home of the Scottish Office—is cool and sophisticated. Designed by Henry Holland with a rather academic portico and a rotunda, it is architecturally immaculate. And it completes perfectly a sequence of façades that should be one of the architectural sights of London. Their modest elevations never soar out of reach of the passer-by, yet they are always changing, always full of character and interest. They demonstrate the supreme, almost effortless, grace and skill of these Georgian town architects.

Opposite, however, is the antithesis. Facing the Horse Guards is the fantastic late-Victorian baroque of the old War Office. It is a huge block on a grand scale. The massive rustication, heavy cornices, stone cupolas on the corner turrets and swags, scrolls and luscious statues in abundance, all tell of a nation at the height of its military pride (it was built in 1898). At this point, Whitehall is almost in danger of losing itself to a rather pompous joke, though the joke has become light and more enjoyable since the block has been transformed by cleaning from black to glistening white.

Behind the War Office is another joke—but a noble one—in Whitehall Court. This massive series of flats and clubs went up in 1884—including the National Liberal Club at the end, by Waterhouse. Recent cleaning has brought out the variety of styles and motifs employed and presented them as not bad buildings at all. But their crowning glory is their skyline, which must have been deliberately intended to stand out in views from across the river and from back in St. James's Park. From a distance their towers, spires and conical turrets look like some enchanted Bavarian castle. Until someone can design a skyline like that, they should never be pulled down—as someone apparently wants to do at present.

Back in Whitehall across Horse Guards Avenue, stands the jewel of the piece: Inigo Jones's Banqueting House. It was built in 1619 as the stylistic climax to the long-vanished Whitehall Palace. Indeed, it was intended merely as the first part of a grand new palace in the Italian or French manner to stretch from the Strand to Westminster. William III's disenchantment with Whitehall air ended all that. Jones's 'new' renaissance style was as shattering a break from contemporary architecture as the Royal Festival Hall is from the Theatre Royal, Haymarket. The very commonplaceness of its classical pillars, cornices and balustrades to us today is an indication of the tremendous and lasting influence of the English Palladian movement of which Jones was the real initiator. And despite its stylistic purity it remains highly individualistic. There is certainly no building in Italy that is like it—though it must be admitted that there is not much English about Rubens's amazing ceiling inside, in breath-taking contrast to Jones's classical restraint.

An even more blazing contrast, however, is represented by the Air Ministry building behind and beyond the Banqueting House—a classic example of the decline in public patronage since the seventeenth century. Its hulking great cubes of philistine concrete might have been transported straight from the banks of the Moscow River. But who will guard our guardians? The Ministry of Public Building was at work.

On the other side of Whitehall, Georgian gives way to Victorian, and domestic restraint to a slightly pompous self-confidence. The Treasury building, however, next to Dover House, is still modest. A simple order of columns runs the whole length of the façade separating the windows, but with a pleasantly ornate cornice—as if Sir Charles Barry, the architect, were eager to show deference to Inigo Jones across the way.

Down Downing Street is the row of eighteenth-century town houses that form what must be the most unobtrusive and restrained set of official residences anywhere in the world. Architecturally they are absolutely straightforward Georgian brick houses—although since No. 10 became the home of the Prime Minister they have been reconstructed inside. Behind Downing Street, through the Treasury Passage, is a warren of ancient architectural survivals—including a few remnants of the days of the Whitehall Palace itself.

Across Downing Street, Sir George Gilbert Scott shows no deference whatsoever to his Georgian forebears in his High Victorian Foreign Office. It is Italianate at its London best—the result of Palmerston's characteristic aversion to the fashionable Gothic for his prized palace of diplomacy. It is an ordered flourish of arches, columns, statues and medallions, but desperately in need of a clean. And the reason why it needs a clean is that the Ministry of Public Building are holding it in the condemned cell for demolition. If they get away with this it would be a tragedy. All one can hope for at present is that some kind Civil Servant will at least allow the old lady to clean herself up a bit before execution so we can see what splendour we are destroying.

Finally on this side, cornering on to Parliament Square, is an echo of the High Victorian baroque of the War Office, now housing a number of government departments. It is not a particularly distinguished building—but it has acquired a certain ponderous charm with age.

Across Whitehall, however, comes the saddest tale of all. For the Ministry of Public Building and Works plan to raze to the ground everything from Richmond Terrace down to Westminster Bridge. In doing so they would destroy not only two priceless buildings but the whole human scale of this great street, which depends for its reassertion on the Georgian and Victorian town houses in Parliament Street. The site includes Richmond Terrace, set at right-angles to Whitehall and the only example of unified Georgian terracing in this part of London. It still has the air of a university town about it—suitable, since it houses part of the Department of Education—and its angular siting is vital to the view down Whitehall at this point. Behind is its mews, still standing and crying out for something imaginative to be done with it.

Beyond it stands—or rises—Norman Shaw's terrifying masterpiece, New Scotland Yard. Its soaring red brick turrets and asymmetrical late-Victorian layout made it a splendid home for the Metropolitan Police, now moved to Victoria Street. It is, from a historical point of view, the only major example of Shaw's official architecture in London—not enough, apparently, to earn it official respect.

In front of New Scotland yard, in Derby Gate, is the fine building of the old Whitehall Club in an aggressively Italian style. And the houses along Parliament Street include many excellent Georgian façades—particularly the stuccoed Post Office. All this is planned to come down—against protests from everyone, including the Greater London Council and the government's own Ministry of Housing and Local Government. But the point surely about Whitehall, even today, is that it is not just a street of government offices, a bureaucratic compound like any capital city in the world. It is a street full of houses in which real people could actually be living, not just faceless men pushing paper. A visit to Whitehall is not a visit to a Kafka-esque wilderness of officialdom, and civil servants themselves should be thankful for it.

Church of St. John in Smith Square.

25-Smith Square

London never experienced the comprehensive replanning of cities such as Paris. In the inner London area, sites were rebuilt as and when commercial needs dictated. And since commercial values tended to be higher on the main streets than behind them, sites on such streets saw the most frequent redevelopment and tend now to contain the larger and more modern blocks. The by-product of this is that in London, again as in few other cities, there are always examples of architectural antiquity to be found immediately behind the most soulless thoroughfares. A classic example of this occurs on Millbank between Westminster Abbey and Lambeth Bridge.

As far as Millbank itself is concerned, some efforts have been made to make it tolerable. Young trees desperately try to breathe along the pavements. Above Abingdon Street garage a little shrubbery is progressing round a small green, sporting a bold, if slightly incongruous, Henry Moore statue. And across the road is a real lung—Victoria Tower Gardens—beneath the west range of the Palace of Westminster. The gardens contain two of London's most excellent statues, one of Emily Pankhurst, and another, a casting of Rodin's Burghers of Calais—both suitably political in the shadow of Parliament. But it is the view of the Victoria Tower that makes these gardens so splendid. This façade is surely one of the most impressive examples of real Victorian architecture in London. Somehow the Perpendicular line of the Tower is just right, set at an angle to the gardens, with the more distant spires showing over the roof and adding a touch of Gothic variety.

Across the river, there is the succession of County Hall, the modern version of St. Thomas's Hospital and the medieval warmth of Lambeth Palace—the London residence of the

Archbishop of Canterbury. They make an inconsistent but lively river frontage, which declines rapidly above Lambeth Bridge. Lambeth Palace in particular, capped by crenellations and surrounded by trees, makes one of the few genuinely Tudor vistas left in inner London. Its centre-piece is the old Great Hall, now containing the library—rebuilt in a rare example of late seventeenth-century Gothic but with a decidedly renaissance lantern tower in the roof. Next to it, Lambeth Bridge returns to Westminster, recently repainted in the Greater London Council's imaginative pop art colouring of bright red and brown.

Back on the embankment stand the cliffs of commercialism. The easternmost, on Abingdon Street, is architecturally speaking not so bad—a brick-and-stone Edwardian block housing the Church Commissioners. But the colossal Crown Agents' and Imperial Chemical Industries' blocks next door are monstrous buildings in which it is impossible to detect any architectural merit whatsoever. They are yet another contribution to the dismal façade London presents to the Thames.

The real gems of this area require a plunge into the back streets. And here lie some of the best preserved early Georgian streets in London. Amongst them is some sensitive infilling by twentieth-century architects aware, for once, of the scale and quality of the neighbourhood in which they were working.

In the middle is Smith Square and in the centre of this stands one of London's most curious architectural treasures—the Church of St. John, heavily bombed in the war and only now acquiring a new lease of life as a community and cultural centre. St. John's is real English baroque—too heavy and grave for eighteenth-century Italy or Germany, but too free and unconventional to be anything but baroque. It is in the form of a rather stunted cross, with four great ornate towers of unique design—reputedly the result of Queen Anne's request to the architect, Thomas Archer, to build a church like her upturned footstool. All the footstool now needs is a good clean.

Smith Square is not what it must once have been. The bombs took their toll and politicians have done the rest. It is hard to say which is worst of Conservative Central Office or Transport House. The Conservatives are more conventional and more in keeping with the proportions of the square; Transport House is more imaginative, but more incongruous.

It is better to keep to the other side of the square where there are some superb early Georgian houses with exquisite porches. All the skill of the designer seems to have been compressed into the door-cases and porch brackets—each one different, but blending into the next. Gayfere Street, leading out of the north-west corner of the square, still contains houses of just two storeys—almost incredible survivals in this part of the city. But the real pride of Westminster is Lord North Street, progressing from Smith Square towards the Abbey. Dating from the 1720s, it represents modest Georgian town housing at its best.

Dominating the northern end is No. 4 Cowley Street—an interesting case of infilling. It is an early twentieth-century Queen Anne style mansion, which while not conforming directly to the scale of the neighbourhood does not completely destroy it. The failure is in the inability of the architect to respect the window line of the adjacent houses, losing that crucial sense of uniformity amid individuality that the Georgians so respected. But the use of similar materials such as red brick with abundant white woodwork maintains the overall character of the street and prevents it from being offensive. The remainder of Cowley Street is an almost miraculous survival, almost entirely early Georgian and gaily decorated with window-boxes and fresh paint. It turns a corner sedately into Barton Street before ending up at Great College Street.

The ancient stone wall in Great College Street signifies the boundary of the Abbey grounds. Into it are set doorways and windows of Tudor—or earlier—proportions, while beyond it looms the dramatic Victoria Tower once again. Most of the buildings in this street belong to Westminster School and through an arch at its western corner Dean's Yard and the main school buildings can be reached, as well as the back entrance to the exquisite cloisters of the Abbey itself.

This whole area, from Smith Square right through to Dean's Yard, is amazingly free of the normal hustle of modern traffic and people. Especially at night, it retains a gentle, eighteenth-century air about it. One might expect, at any moment, a hansom cab rather than a modern taxi to come round the next corner.

A house in Belgrave Square.

West London

26-Belgrave Square

Thomas Cubitt's Belgravia ranks with John Nash's Regent's Park as one of London's two great contributions to European town architecture. Cubitt followed close on Nash's heels, starting to fill in the marshy fields behind the new Buckingham Palace with soil excavated from St. Katharine's Dock near the Tower of London at the same time as Nash was commencing his grand sweep of terraces north of St. Marylebone. And like Nash he was driven on by a supreme confidence in the viability of a property speculation that would make most present-day tycoons quake with insecurity.

Belgravia, however, not being developed under royal patronage like the Park, was a tighter, more 'commercial' venture, without Nash's lavish scenic gestures. Cubitt was first and foremost a builder and businessman. Today he would doubtless be throwing up skyscrapers, experimenting with new techniques of construction and engaging in lavish office speculations. In the mid nineteenth century, he was mercifully operating within an architectural vernacular that was perfectly suited to the civilised manner in which the city was developing and the residential needs of the people for whom he was building. Cubitt was not an artist with buildings—a phrase that could certainly be applied to Nash in Regent's Park. He was an exceptionally competent draughtsman with a superb sense of scale who knew what he was doing down to the last door-knob. And he came on to the scene just when he was needed. His Belgravia stands today, virtually intact, as a characteristic English blend of the stately and the picturesque, with grand squares and peaceful backwaters, firm grid-like Georgian terracing and bold sweeping crescents, stately vistas and sudden visual surprises.

Before tackling Belgravia itself, one little Cubitt set-piece in

Knightsbridge is worth noting by way of an *hors-d'œuvre*. It is Albert Gate, two blocks built by Cubitt in 1845. At one time they were known as Malta and Gibraltar, because people were convinced 'they would never be taken'. They are two superb Italianate *palazzi* standing either side of the gate, magnificently opulent and bold with two delicate bronze deer marking the entrance into the park. The west one was finally taken by the railway magnate George Hudson; that on the east is the French embassy and contained the first mechanical lift in London.

Although many people had a hand in various sections of the Belgravia development—which eventually stretched from Knightsbridge right down to the river at Pimlico—it seems likely that the overall layout was by Thomas Cundy, architect to the Grosvenor estate who were the originators of the whole scheme. Cubitt himself, apart from being the progenitor and backer, designed many of the individual terraces—but not Belgrave Square itself—and his huge construction company carried out all the actual building.

The best way to approach Belgravia is from the north down Wilton Crescent, the only street faced in stone rather than white stucco. This is London's answer to Edinburgh's New Town, though being later in date it is more fussy, less restrained. The balustrade along the roof of the Crescent, for instance, suddenly swoops down a floor at each corner, making a weak stylistic gimmick out of an otherwise strong line. But the balconies and railings and the severe grey stone make a splendid curve down to the lightness and grandeur of Belgrave Square. Down behind the east limb of Wilton Crescent is a classic English contrast: the 'Grenadier' pub. Quaint and surrounded by trees it really might be tucked away in the country somewhere.

The entrance to the Square from this side of Wilton Crescent is a barrage of architectural sensations. Grosvenor Crescent curves suddenly back towards Hyde Park Corner, with a bow-fronted house on the corner facing diagonally out into the square, Halkin Street shoots off to the left, and Belgrave Square itself stretches out ahead and to the right like an open pair of compasses. And over it all is the tremendous impression of space created by the massed trees in the square.

Belgrave Square was designed by a young architect called George Basevi. It is one of the largest and certainly the grandest in

London. Each side, in true Georgian style, was conceived as a unified composition, with central bays emphasised by pilasters or portico and, in one case, by a remarkably ornate pediment. The traditional Georgian restraint was gradually giving away, in these years, to the more florid Italianate style of the mid-nineteenth century. This can be seen in the subtle variations between the different sides of the square—both in the treatment of the central sections and in the design of the windows and porches. Whereas a pre-Regency architect would have been happy to have had them all the same, Basevi sought restless variations—a rather pointless exercise since few people would normally realise that each side is different from all the others.

But the real ingenuity in Belgrave Square is in the way the difficult corners are treated—difficult because the development demanded two streets leading at right-angles from each one. To mitigate the weakness this creates, large detached mansions, each set in its own garden and designed by different architects, are placed diagonally across the square. They neatly slice each corner, without making it so weak that the eye is led out of the square, nor so tight that the square seems too enclosed. It is picturesque planning at its best.

The development stretched on down across the Kings Road, through Eaton Place and Square and Chester Square to Warwick and Eccleston Squares. The latter two are now no longer Belgravia but Pimlico, ruthlessly segregated by the railway line to Victoria which was built later. Ebury Street, running through the middle, is a low-key contrast—small-scale terraced housing and shops, a sort of service road to the great estate. As a result, it survives today with a remarkable number of single-occupancy houses inhabited by the sort of people whose servants would have lived in them a century ago.

The varied execution of the overall plan by individual clients can be seen in streets such as Eaton Place and Eaton Square—not so much a square as two very long terraces set back behind gardens from the Kings Road. These gardens, incidentally, contain some fine modern British sculpture. Some houses, or indeed whole terraces, are in the grand Italian style, while others are more straightforward late-Georgian with pilasters and plain windows, some have huge cornices, others pompous balustrades. Most are stuccoed, but some have their walls in bare brick.

Running between the main streets and squares are their respective mews, now mosly converted to smaller and more manageable houses. These are the unique possessions of a city that was prosperous and spacious enough to build itself suburbs in the days when people still travelled on horseback and owned their own carriages. They are also, it should be added, the result of a system of leasehold tenure that preserves them for a century at a time from redevelopment. One of the more interesting features of so many of the Belgravia mews is their ingenious and often highly ornate gatehouses, such as those in Eccleston Street and Lyall Street.

Down the western side of the development run smaller streets in the direction of the older Hans Town across the top end of Sloane Street. Most of the original Lowndes Square has now been destroyed—its pleasant northern range has only recently been pulled down—but Kinnerton, Motcomb, West Halkin and Lowndes Streets remain, full of antique shops and smart restaurants. And although they do not achieve the almost rural atmosphere of the Montpelier Square neighbourhood farther on in Knightsbridge, they retain, with their attendant lanes and mews, the feel of a village within a town which is so unique to London. In Motcomb Street still stands the stately old Pantechnicon designed like a Greek Doric temple, once a great auction room and now being rebuilt behind its original façade for the same purpose.

But the most remarkable thing about Belgravia is its sheer survival. Thanks for this must go partly to the lasting excellence of Cubitt's original building work—always first-rate in contrast to Nash's shoddiness. Partly also to the fact that enough individuals and a few institutions have been able to afford to live in so expensive a neighbourhood continuously over the years. The size of the houses has meant that conversion to flats has been easier than in earlier and smaller developments. The menace of offices has thus been kept at bay.

Much of Belgravia has recently been renovated and restuccoed. The result, particularly on a sunny day with a blue sky, is an almost Mediterranean blaze of whiteness, regularly relieved by the ubiquitous London plane-trees which seem to burst out of every gap. It is all a magnificent neighbourhood, and a standing refutation of those who maintain that London is all dull and grey. Belgravia is neither—and, with luck, never will be.

27-Pont Street Dutch

Ask most people what happened to London architecture between the Victorian Gothic revival and present-day modernism and they will not be able to answer. If pressed, they would probably assume that those grim nineteenth-century monstrosities and florid Italianate terraces slid gradually into boring twentieth-century neo-Georgian blocks and mock-Tudor suburban dwellings. And broadly speaking they would be right. The years from 1890 to 1950 were not happy ones in the story of London's buildings. First there was the money to redevelop, but not the taste—and so much that was good was destroyed. And then, after the first world war, there was not even the money.

But there were, nevertheless, rays of light, and one such ray was the work of architects associated with the name of Richard Norman Shaw. In a sense they represented a new type of architect. Not for them the opportunities of a Nash or a Cubitt. They did not have vast estates and tracts of open land to develop, nor were they speculators on a grand scale, building long terraces and then selling or leasing units within it. The architects of the seventies and eighties found themselves mostly 'infilling', designing single houses or groups of houses on existing estates chiefly for individual clients.

Perhaps because of this, they reverted to a style that was neither the grandiloquent classicism that characterised both Nash and Cubitt's work forty years earlier, nor the passionate Gothic of the contemporary church-builders. Their style was individual and domestic, the style of the seventeenth- and early eighteenth-century Dutch, Jacobean and Queen Anne architects.

Examples of their work are inevitably scattered and it is hard to do them justice by reference to individual streets as such. But

Pont Street Dutch in Harrington Gardens

the fact that they did not design in the fashionable classical or Gothic styles, and that they were building a mere ninety years ago, should not detract from an appreciation of their quality which is worth every bit as much attention as that of more popular styles. For the domestic buildings of Shaw, and contemporaries such as J. J. Stevenson, Sir Ernest George and Peto, revived a style that had infinitely more individuality, colour and warmth than the coldly elegant mid-Victorian uniformity they supplanted. And their buildings have the added quality of being immense fun to look at.

The best known, if not the best, examples of this period are the streets of the Cadogan estate in Chelsea, round Hans Crescent and Cadogan Square, through which runs Pont Street—hence Osbert Lancaster's christening of the style, Pont Street Dutch.

The area was first laid out back in the eighteenth century as an early exercise in town planning by Henry Holland, the great Georgian architect, and was known as Hans Town. However, in the 1880s it was comprehensively rebuilt with large town houses for the wealthy of that most wealthy of periods, and in the grounds of Holland's old 'Pavilion' rose the extraordinary Cadogan Square.

The essential features of the Dutch revival can best be seen in Hans Crescent. Once this was a dramatic sweep of Georgian houses. Now with a few survivals and a few new blocks, it is an energetic succession of red brick and terracotta house, no two the same and all striving to outdo the next in individuality. Most have heavily gabled roofs, heavily mullioned—almost Tudor—windows, lots of balconies and railings often at different levels to break any horizontal line, and a multitude of early renaissance motifs.

Up in Hans Road beyond, the style got quite out of hand in Harrods' terracotta. The rear entrance, facing Walton Place, is a fantastic monster portal of jumbled motifs, capped absurdly by a water-tank. Just across from it, however, are three museum pieces —Nos. 14–16 and No. 12 Hans Road—built in the 1890s. The first is by Voysey and the second by A. H. Mackmurdo and both make intriguing comparisons with the boldly self-confident Dutch styles on either side. They were architects seemingly searching for a style—the Voysey pair, in particular, being strongly horizontal in line with oriel windows and Arts and Crafts motifs round the doors: almost like a set of artisans cottages stacked on top of one another. Yet neither style really developed and these survivals remain as sad examples of an architectural cul-de-sac.

Back through Hans Crescent and into Pont Street, the red brick gables rise and fall with mounting tension. St. Columba's Church, filling the western corner of the street, complements this splendidly with its weird white tower and roof. And the recent cleaning of some of the houses, which previously were an unattractive sooty orange, has helped greatly in bringing out the vigorous red which is so characteristic of the style.

It is worth walking a few yards to Walton Street just to see what fifty years had done to London domestic architecture. The dazzling white stucco of the Italianate mansions cornering Beauchamp Place just could not be more of a contrast; the uniform terrace to the right towards Harrods is graceful and restrained—everything Pont Street Dutch most certainly is not.

Down to Cadogan Square, the Dutch goes grand and loses some of its charm. Massive terracotta colonnades stretch across a number of façades, trying unsuccessfully to play a game the classicists played much better. The supports for the balconies become gross, and the nice, intimate porches of Hans Crescent reach massive proportions. But they are all still fascinating buildings. Massed along the skyline, they possess a tense, restless harmony.

The same style but with completely different atmosphere is buried down among the mid-Victorian terraces and once-grand squares of South Kensington and Earls Court. In Collingham Gardens and Harrington Gardens lies a small group of buildings designed by the firm of Sir Ernest George & Peto that might, with a bit of imagination, have come straight from the quays of Amsterdam or Bruges. The contrast of these houses with the surrounding stucco classicism, built not much earlier, is extraordinary. Gone are the grand porches of 'South Ken' pomposity. Here are diminutive Jacobean doorways, welcoming rather than forbidding. 35–7 Harrington Gardens has magnificent ironwork railings, tall, light first-floor windows surmounted by delicious carvings and high gables on the steep hipped roof. Next door, built for the composer W. S. Gilbert, the Dutch goes wild. Floors two, three and four are built into a massive Flemish stepped gable and the porch, placed to one side, is a delightful piece of brick and stone Jacobean.

Beyond, the gables, projecting windows and balustrades jumble the perspective as far as No. 45, where some later and unsuccessful imitations take over until Collingham Gardens is reached.

Collingham Gardens, similarly gabled, is set round a central garden. Each house is different—often strikingly so. Some have red and white brick patterned walls, others intricate terracotta window and door surrounds. Some are heavily mannerist in style, others remarkably pure late-Tudor. Some have a plain flat façade, others advance and recede round courtyards with projecting oriel windows. At No. 12a, there is a huge joke of a balcony, requiring huge ornate brackets to support it. The architects must have had immense fun with these buildings, searching their pattern-books for ever-more extraordinary motifs. Yet they never lost control. Always the scale is down-beat, domestic and human. For once houses are being designed for people to feel at home in.

There are many other examples of Dutch revivalism, though no equivalent concentration. Shaw's Swan House on the Embankment is one, as is his brilliantly influential 196 Queen's Gate. Many are out of favour and neglected. Many desperately need cleaning—red brick and terracotta look frightful when dirty. Many, like the fascinating row of gables at the top end of Brompton Road, will doubtless soon be destroyed. But one day we shall treasure them as we now treasure the classical and Gothic revivals. And we shall regret our present neglect.

Rutland Street, off the Brompton Road.

28-Montpelier Square

An illusion of rural living in the centre of towns is a goal which urban architects have sought to achieve ever since cities began to grow beyond their defensive walls. Every man wants his castle—or at least his house, his garden and a view of grass and trees. Where sufficient land is available, the suburb is the commonest answer. But in town centres, the cost of land and the accessibility of common services demands a much higher density of houses. London's answer to this problem was the town square, basically comprising four coherent terraces of houses set round a central garden and secluded from any main thoroughfare. There are many examples, but one of the most characteristic is Montpelier Square in Knightsbridge. With its surrounding neighbourhood, it forms one of the most delightful residential backwaters in London.

Montpelier Square, with adjacent Trevor Square, are in a typically favoured position. They are sandwiched in the triangle between the thoroughfares of Brompton Road and Knightsbridge and have been insulated from commercial development by the ribbon principle operating along the main roads to Kensington. Properties on these roads could be redeveloped over and again to yield even higher returns as warehouses, shops and offices. But the buildings behind have remained residential throughout.

The Trevor and Montpelier estates were built as speculations in the late eighteenth and early nineteenth centuries on the high land beyond Knightsbridge Green. The air was regarded as free from the city fumes and the fields enjoyed excellent views south across the Thames Valley—hence the fashionable continental name, Montpelier. The slope down from the hill can best be seen in Trevor Square and Place, where beautiful Georgian Terraces drop down from the Knightsbridge heights. Alas, today the slope ends bang up against the foot of Harrods' massive terracotta warehouse. The Edwardian residents of Trevor Place must have said a thing or two when that went up!

Trevor Square itself, the first development in the area, is an idyllic oasis of domestic calm, just a few paces from the roar of Brompton Road. Little alleyways with gas-lamps lead off to the shops of Knightsbridge Green and through into Trevor Place. The turn from Trevor Place itself into Montpelier Square is marked by larger and later houses with white stucco and pilasters. The scale of the square is much grander, built as it was some twenty years later than Trevor Place at the beginning of the Victorian age. It has lost the latter's stricter Georgian uniformity although it is still basically Georgian in style. The houses have four storeys instead of three. The windows have Italianate surrounds and the doorways and balconies are more individualistic. But one of the chief pleasures of Montpelier Square is its trees and general greenery. They are packed into the central garden giving the square an illusion of much greater size. Many of the houses also have luxuriant creeper growing up the walls.

South from the calm of the square, Montpelier Street appears to glide away down to Brompton Road. The houses reduce to three-storey local shops, and the curve of the street gives a sense of long perspective to what is really a very short link—a perfect example of casual Georgian town-planning.

South of the square is a maze of minor streets and mews. The Georgian town cottage style of Sterling Street, and of Montpelier Place and Walk, achieves an atmosphere which is no less refreshing for having become 'chic'. Then suddenly one is not in the centre of West London at all but in some Cornish seaside town, with two-storey terraces in white or pastel-coloured plaster. They are totally unsophisticated but never mean, as similar ones often seem elsewhere. Could anyone, set down in Rutland Street with its creeper-covered houses, maritime bow-windows and pokey little brick cottages, ever believe they were just 200 yards from Harrods?

But the strangest sensation is yet to come. For looming over one end of Rutland Street is the back side of one of the neighbouring estates—Rutland Square, with beyond it the back of Brompton Square and Ennismore Gardens. These later squares were developed totally distinct from Montpelier and Trevor Squares.

Rutland Gate and Ennismore Gardens were designed in the high Victorian Italianate style typical of west London, and were planned as leading off Knightsbridge to the north, just as Brompton Square leads off Brompton Road to the south.

The fascinating result of this disjointed development is that the mews quarters for these grand squares had to fit in as best they could between the backs of the main houses—and have now become valuable residential backwaters. The only direct link, for instance, between the Montpelier and Rutland Gate neighbourhoods is a flight of steps in a wall in Rutland Street. They lead straight into the courtyard of Rutland Mews East—in a late Regency style that is strongly reminiscent of Spain. Rutland Mews West, next door, with its own gate and private yard, would certainly be at home in Seville. This lane leads on past stately views north to Rutland Gate and Ennismore Gardens and through a pompous set of Victorian pillars into the gardens and cobbled mews behind Brompton Oratory.

This little quarter, indeed, is almost impossible to categorise. One moment it seems charming, almost idyllic—the next it is all quite fantastic. What on earth, for instance, is that massive Italian cathedral, Brompton Oratory, doing soaring up over the pure English plane-trees? And how is it cheek by jowl with the utterly Anglican neo-Gothic of Holy Trinity, Brompton, just behind it? Mews and alleys seem to shoot off in every direction, and traffic is almost totally absent. It is like a wonderful daydream.

For all London's great works of architecture, it is areas like this that are truly unique. They have arisen piecemeal as a result of the city's curious historical development. And although no one building may seem in itself particularly important—or worth last-ditch preservation—the total collection of houses, streets, squares and alleyways form together a composition of the greatest architectural value.

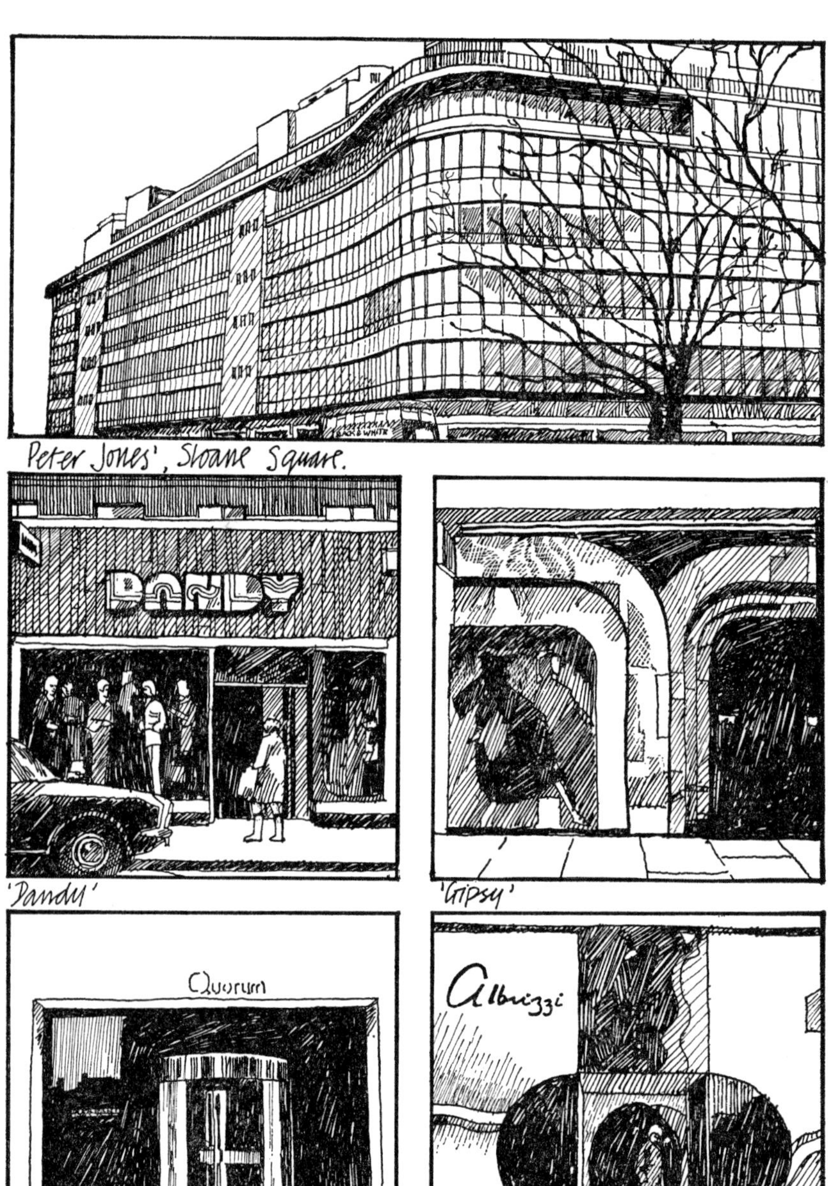

'Peter Jones', Sloane Square.

'Dandy'

'Gipsy'

'Quorum'.

'Albrizzi', Kings Road.

29-King's Road

The King was Charles II, and the road was a footpath enlarged into a private way to facilitate his passage from St. James's Palace to Hampton Court. It remained private until the reign of George IV.

The real trouble with the King's Road today is that it has retained this original function—that of being the main route southwest out of London. For it is at present going through a period of being one of the most fascinating streets in London—at least in human terms. Indeed, so crowded and self-absorbed has it become that even the ubiquitous traffic has been subjugated by the pedestrians—a rare thing to happen in any city street.

But the fascination of the King's Road is not just that of eccentric shops and perpetual visual titillation. It is also that this road happens to be one of the most successful, if fortuitous, pieces of town environment in London. It forms the wavy spine of a neighbourhood whose piecemeal development has resulted in a harmonious succession of squares, terraces, alleys and cul-de-sacs. It might all be a perfect exercise in making big city living tolerable—were it not for the traffic.

The upper part of the King's Road is not important to its character. It is part of Belgravia (Chapter 26). The true 'Road' is heralded by Sloane Square. There is something extraordinary about this Square—just a jumble of late nineteenth- and early twentieth-century buildings, yet with tremendous character. The secret perhaps lies in the trees and the coloured lights that fill them at night—achieving the nearest London has to a Parisian *place*. Then there is the *avant garde* Royal Court Theatre and Sloane Square underground station, the only one serving Chelsea and thus generating masses of people. But the real prize of Sloane

Square is Peter Jones. This was one of London's first really exciting pieces of new architecture, built back in 1936. Its curving line beckons the eye out of Sloane Square down into Chelsea, modern, self-confident and totally lasting. It might have been designed yesterday (but compare it with the contemporary *Daily Express* building in Fleet Street).

The first fifty yards of King's Road are already in danger of losing some of their traditional character. On the right-hand side are now nothing but places to eat or be clothed, and most of these have too much capital behind them to be truly 'Chelsea'. However, the risk of blandness is mitigated by the sense of space provided opposite by the Duke of York's headquarters, complete with austere portico and colourful Chelsea pensioners on the seats outside. Perhaps one day the public will be allowed inside to rest tired feet on the expanse of grass. If only the railings could be removed, the sense of place added to this part of Chelsea would be immense. And the yellow brick of the sensible Victorian buildings in King's Road itself deserves greater emphasis. Come on, Army, open up a bit.

Just beyond, however, comes a nine-storey block of flats, which has a disastrous effect on the scale not just of this part of the King's Road but on all views up it from the west. One day, we shall be strong-minded enough to pull down such eyesores.

A few yards farther down comes the new heart of Chelsea, successor to Sloane Square: the Sainsbury's precinct and Royal Avenue. Royal Avenue is very old indeed, conceived back in the seventeenth century when Christopher Wren built the Royal Hospital—the British 'Invalides'—and planned a tree-lined avenue leading from it right through to Kensington Palace. The avenue, planted with plane-trees on either side, never reached farther than the King's Road, where it now yields to a devilish cross-traffic before plunging into the new precinct and a maze of chic side-streets.

The view of the Hospital itself is magnificent. The whole composition—trees, grass, long vistas, red brick, stone and stucco portico and slate roof—is a perfect civilised townscape. The plan to block off the top end of Royal Avenue should also grant peace to this excellent contrast with the garishness of the modern King's Road.

Back, however, on the Road is the womb-like Sainsbury's

precinct with its highly suggestive sculpture. It dips down slightly from the road level and is all suitably intimate and friendly—an excellent piece of town design. Opposite stands the brilliantly bizarre Drugstore, smaller in scale and thus far more exciting than its Parisian counterparts. Its basically classical outline is only marred by the absurd retention of the original neo-Dutch two storeys on top—but then that's the King's Road all over.

By now, the King's Road's most important feature is beginning to show itself—the curve of its line. Looking west from the Drugstore the view down the road is broken frequently by distinctive buildings seen at an angle, and, just as vital, by frequent splashes of green jutting out from the squares. All this turns the street into a succession of places, rather than just a thoroughfare.

Below Royal Avenue, Wellington and Markham Squares are further examples of urban seclusion cheek by jowl with the jangling sensations of the Road itself. On the corner of Markham Square, the new Barclays Bank provides an excellent example of careful, sensitive, infilling: modern but respectfully three-storeyed, precisely what is needed.

On the right, just past Markham Square is the bizarre Graeco-Roman entrance to the Old Pheasantry—now a discotheque—topped by a miniature quadriga, and surrounded by a galaxy of coloured lights, bad restaurants and exasperated traffic. In the side-streets behind, in Markham and Godfrey Streets, is colourful Chelsea cottage architecture—full of assorted styles and motifs.

Farther on, there is a sudden interlude, provided by a cinema and the ponderous Chelsea Town Hall. The King's Road seems almost in danger of becoming respectable. Indeed to the right up Sydney Street is one of the most respectable buildings in Chelsea—St. Luke's Church. This is a fine example of early Gothic revival, mercifully surrounded by expansive gardens. Its tremendous proportions—in the Perpendicular style—complete with flying buttresses and weatherbeaten Tudor tower, stand stark and bold, only mitigated by a warm stone of almost Cotswold texture.

Back in the King's Road, just past Oakley Street, is the charming early eighteenth-century Argyle House, followed by a row of Georgian houses which deserve better than to be hidden by a necessarily high fence from the roar of traffic past their front doors. Opposite are Chelsea Fire Station and the College of Science and Technology, both enterprising modern buildings which none-the-less preserve the scale of this part of the Road. Their best feature is perhaps their subdued texture—in grey and white concrete and cement—which is lasting so much better than on many similar buildings.

Almost immediately, however, the true King's Road reasserts itself. Carlyle Square and Paulton's Square repeat the sedate diversions provided earlier by Wellington and Markham Squares. And the shops here are those that might have been found half a mile farther up five years ago. The antique shops are not altogether ruinous, there are still a few grocery stores and there is the fascinating antique supermarket. Then, just past the leafy suburban Vale, the King's Road takes a sharp kink to the left, with some exotic shopfronts ahead which must distract many a motorist to near disaster.

It is, however, the Road's last fling. For as it straightens out towards the famous World's End pub, the lesson which still must be learnt about such streets becomes plain. A planner has seized its gently curving line and created a cold straight one of shops with flats above. It is fatal and World's End itself—one of London's great pubs—stands at the end, stark and isolated. The imaginative spirit is still there—Chelsea 'colonies' crop up occasionally farther on. But somehow the soul has been lost. Towards Fulham, the King's Road comes up against the West Cross Route and suburbia. And that is that.

30-Cheyne Walk

But before embarking upon Cheyne Walk itself, it is worth noticing some houses just to its east on Chelsea Embankment. These houses, and others in Swan Walk and Tite Street behind, were built in the late-Victorian period. Their stylistic moving spirit was Norman Shaw and his Swan House (No. 17) is a classic work of urbane, refined good taste. The inspiration is clearly Jacobean—the overhanging floors, the first floor oriel windows giving ample natural light and the decorative surrounds. Yet the treatment is perfectly modern—the doors, for instance, are pure Arts and Crafts movement in design. The building, incidentally, now houses Securicor and is bristling with hidden eyes and other devices—protection, we can only hope, against demolition men as much as burglars. The other houses in this area are less significant, but make a similar use of bay windows and recesses, red brick and white paint—full of movement and style and never dull.

Cheyne Walk, however, is a different matter. Life must have been bliss to its early inhabitants. Their splendid terrace houses, much bigger than those of their contemporaries in Westminster, extended out east and west of the old Chelsea Church, with fields behind them and the river in front. A few older Tudor and Jacobean mansions were also spread out on either side along the river.

The building of the Chelsea Embankment in the nineteenth century changed all that, helped by the dramatic expansion southwards of the suburb of Kensington. But the thoughtfulness of the early builders in leaving themselves some space from the river-bank at least meant that the new road did not go right past the front doors. For all the terrific noise and vibration to which Cheyne Walk is now subjected it still has a secluded air about it.

Number Four, Cheyne Walk.

Mostly set behind an assortment of small gardens, walls and railings, its houses have always seemed graceful and elegant—despite the raffish reputations of many of their past inhabitants.

The initial row of the Walk, leading off the west end of Royal Hospital Road, contains some of the largest and finest early Georgian houses in London. Nos. 3–6 are in gently ascending order of grandness. No. 4 was the home of the novelist, George Eliot and is a classic early Georgian combination of red and brown brick with white stucco. No. 5 has gateposts worthy of the entrance to a country estate and No. 6 has some intriguing Oriental eighteenth-century railings. All have excellent doorways set firmly into the middle of the front—a bold sign of opulence, since this normally meant a width of two rooms rather than one on each floor. Nos. 19–26 are later, about 1760, in place of the old Chelsea Manor. They show their comparative youth by more uniform brown brick and white wood façades and by their doors which are now more modestly pushed to one side of the façade.

Cheyne Mews, down beside No. 23, is pure rural delight, especially in the spring. And coming out of it gives the best view of Albert Bridge, which suddenly bursts above the trees to the right. It is still one of the few real bridges in London—Waterloo and Tower Bridges are others. It does not cross the river, it leaps it, suspended in a graceful arc directly from each of its two ornate towers.

Here, however, is all noise and traffic and computerised lights—and the tragedy of the old pub on the corner now destroyed. But Cheyne Walk plunges back again into the trees at Nos. 38–9—two fascinating early twentieth-century houses by C. R. Ashbee. They are a sort of asymmetrical Georgian revival, with marvellous great studio windows at the back—visible from Oakley Street—and some railings in the style of C. R. Mackintosh in front. Opposite in the gardens, stands a statue (by Boehm) of that *eminence grise* of this part of Chelsea, Carlyle, apparently clad in a dressing-gown.

After a momentary aberration in twentieth-century flats at Shrewsbury House, the scale is restored by more small Georgian houses and the pleasant King's Head and Eight Bells pub—leading up into Cheyne Row. This quarter achieves the almost impossible in that the smaller eighteenth-century houses dominate the larger modern blocks and set the character of the whole neighbourhood. Incredibly there is a hideous Peabody Estate hidden in among them. The most important part is the west side of Cheyne Row itself, dating from the early eighteenth century, roughly contemporary with Queen Anne's Gate. Carlyle lived at No. 24—which is now a museum to his memory. And farther down the Catholic Church of Our Most Holy Redeemer now stands—itself a cosy little piece of neo-Renaissance design (1895) which looks quite stylish amongst all the smart Chelsea cottages. It is worth noting how crucial to the feel of this street is the survival of No. 3 Upper Cheyne Row, directly ahead. Its vertical Georgian proportions add a wonderful sense of elegance to its surroundings.

Back in Cheyne Walk, the Old Church closes the view to the west. This is the heart of old Chelsea, sadly destroyed by bombs in the war and never really revived. The church has been rebuilt to look curiously post-war, although it still contains some superb sixteenth-century monuments. In front is a good, direct statue of Sir Thomas More, Chelsea's most distinguished Tudor resident, looking steadfastly out into the traffic. But the real trouble with this area is the new green—sunken to provide seclusion but merely disappearing from view and emphasising the blank façade of a block of modern flats beyond. Here was the spot for some jumbled, chaotic infilling—not the cold planner's ruler and compasses. The place is bleak, unfriendly and utterly unmemorable. Will the planners never learn?

Beyond, however, still on Cheyne Walk and on the site of Sir Thomas More's Beaufort House, sits Crosby Hall—now part of a students' hostel. It is an architectural transplant from Bishopsgate and is the sole surviving example of the great medieval halls that the fifteenth-century merchants built themselves in the City of London, rivalling the splendour of the commercial competitors elsewhere in Europe. Today it seems soft and comfortably quaint, but in its day it must have been a veritable palace compared with the wattle-and-daub hovels that would have surrounded it. Beyond it across the garden is an ugly block of flats called, with massive presumption, More's Garden.

Past Battersea Bridge, Cheyne Walk enters upon its artistic finale, with the painted barges on the shore and a view of Lots Road power station in the distance. The old Battersea Bridge that so inspired Whistler and Turner is gone. But to the right are some excellent late-Georgian houses they would have known well.

One with a Venetian window beautifully turns the corner of Beaufort Street, and No. 92 next door has a distinguished doorcase and fanlight.

Beyond it is Lindsey House, the only remaining of the grand pre-eighteenth-century riverside mansions of Chelsea. Its residents have included Whistler and the great engineer, Brunel. It was built in about 1674 and would originally have been a plain brick house eleven bays wide and of three storeys. It is now subdivided, stuccoed and with an eighteenth-century Mansard roof. This may have deprived it of its former individuality but it remains a distinguished survivor on the Cheyne Walk scene. Turner lived farther down, at No. 118.

Cheyne Walk finally peters out in a cloud of traffic fumes and desolation, waiting for the passage of the new West Cross Route motorway. The area beyond is solely for the dedicated urban archaeologists. It was once Cremorne Gardens, off which Handel first conducted his famous Water Music Suite. Today it is a wilderness of rubble and warehouses leading into the power station and gasworks. Buried inside the latter, however, stands a fantastic relic. It is Sandford House, literally sheltering under the shadow of a gasholder. It has been much altered since the late seventeenth century when it was built—so legend relates—for Nell Gwynn, whose compelling allure drove Charles II to construct the King's Road to get to her. Today it is derelict and unbelievably sad—indeed it can only be peered at from over the top of a high gate. But it has about it a tremendous sense of architectural romance.

Conclusion

If urban architecture is to be considered an art form, then the art that is enshrined in the streets of London is a highly transient one. For whereas a single building represents a manifestation of an architectural idea which is solid and lasting—often horribly so—the streets of a healthy and developing city can change radically from one year to the next. And in that change, the relationship of old as well as new buildings to one another will alter and the qualities they bring to their environment be enhanced or diminished. It is because of this 'dynamic' aspect of London street architecture that all those who care for seeing its character maintained—indeed who care for the idiosyncratic identity of London itself—must be continually on their guard.

Towards the end of the 1960s the fate of a number of London streets became something of a *cause célèbre* because of the approval of plans for the destruction of certain crucial buildings along their line and the construction of new ones that drastically altered their character. By the middle of 1969, public opinion had been roused as it seldom had been before by proposals for Woburn Square and Bloomsbury Square in Bloomsbury, for Carlton Mews and for Whitehall. And at the same time a series of running battles were being fought over places such as Bishopsgate, Guildhall, Hyde Park Corner and Queen's Gate. The interesting feature of most of these cases was that the authorities responsible were not private developers but agencies of government or public institutions. For these bodies were still able to circumvent, or exert influence to bend, the normal restrictions which have been built up to protect London's architectural environment since the war. Government departments, such as the Ministry of Public Building and Works, can operate well outside the constraints usually imposed on private developers. And institutions such as the University of London and the British Museum can always argue that they are acting for the greater public good in re-developing areas which would be preserved were the motivation a purely commercial one. It is perhaps because these authorities are public ones that their actions in altering the London scene have suddenly become of such great public interest. Indeed, it could be argued that where many people might accept the erection of an ugly new block in place of a charming set of Georgian houses in the name of economic progress, they are far less happy about it when it is being done with their money and in their name.

However, the public battles of 1969 were merely an indication of a deeper change of public attitude that has been developing over a number of years. I recently found myself face to face at a public function with one of those public servants with whom one has often longed to enter the lists over a particular planning decision. In this case it was a man who had been chairman of a planning committee that had, ten years ago, approved the construction of a new block that completely wrecked the scale of a reasonably charming London street. His defence was that at the time the balance of argument had seemed different. The existing buildings on the site were uneconomic and of no architectural merit in themselves. The new designs seemed modern and original. And, most important, planners in those days just did not think in terms of the relationship between a building and a whole street—or at least, did not think it to be an important consideration. It would, he agreed, have been different if the application had come forward today.

Even the most cursory glance at early post-war planning legislation would show that these excuses were at best half-truths. Back in the dim days of 1951, the Ministry of Town and Country Planning was stating in remarkably clear terms the definitions of amenity that should be considered in all planning applications. And throughout the 1950s and 1960s, bodies such as the Historic Buildings Board of the London County Council were fighting often ferocious battles within the planning bureaucracy to preserve not just particular buildings but the character of whole streets. Since streets such as Doughty Street and John Street in Holborn have not been pulled down and are standing more or less intact, it is difficult to realise quite how great was the struggle that went into preserving them. But what is certainly true—and this is where the planning committee chairman was right—is that it is only in the last four or five years that a real head of steam has built up behind the urban conservation movement and widespread concern been expressed by large numbers of people at the way in which the scale and character of cities such as London are being affected by re-development.

In one sense, this heightened awareness has been the result of concerted efforts by particular individuals and groups. Duncan Sandys, with his Civic Amenities Act of 1967, and Richard Crossman during his time at the Ministry of Housing (when he seized historic-buildings protection from the Ministry of Public Building) have played a major part in drawing up a new legislative and administrative framework. Organisations such as the Civic Trust have done immense good work by issuing, and publicising, design awards as well as initiating rehabilitation schemes intended to raise the standards of urban conservation. And the pressure-groups themselves—such as the Society for the Preservation of Ancient Buildings, the Georgian Group and the Victorian Society—have experienced dramatic increases in numbers, reflecting not only increased public interest but also the wider consultative role given them under conservation legislation.

The increased enthusiasm for participation generally has also given a new twist to many planning enquiries and has led to a considerable overspill from self-interested pressure groups into the conservation and historic buildings field. Many people, for instance, who were opposed to the location of a third London airport at Stansted, discovered—some of them doubtless for the first time—that there were some extremely fine architecture and outstanding natural amenities in their neighbourhood. Where previously they had simply disliked the idea of increased noise and traffic invading their community, they now found it politic to campaign on grounds of 'loss of amenity and potential damage to buildings of historic interest'. The same has been broadly true of opposition to the urban motorway proposals of the Greater London Council, especially in areas such as Greenwich. When people feel that technological development is getting the better of them it is to the conservation lobby that they have been turning for help—however far off the main line of their particular interest such help may be.

It is also possible to detect a wider change in taste that may be of even greater significance to public attitudes to town development—and to architectural fashions generally. The late sixties saw a popular revulsion against the conventional architectural wisdom of the day that has already had dramatic impact on attitudes to public housing. The tower blocks of flats erected over the past two decades, particularly in areas such as the East End of London, have proved so inhuman and destructive of neighbourhood relations that people are simply refusing to live in them. A type of accommodation that may be admirably suited to middle-class urban living, where social ties are less geared to geographical proximity, has proved quite unsuited to communities used to the communal intimacy but physical privacy of traditional back-to-back housing. People did not like the architecturally exciting products of modern local housing departments. Only now are we at last seeing—in such developments as those at Lillington Street in Pimlico and Reporton Road in Fulham—a new form of low-rise high density housing that is proving remarkably successful in human terms. And even in the field of middle-class housing, there can be detected a movement towards revivalism and against originality that is alarming to anyone interested in the health of architectural innovation. Not only is the interest in, and value of, Georgian and early Victorian town houses increasing dramatically as people come to appreciate, even more than they always have done, the intrinsic humanity of Georgian architectural proportioning, but the new estates that are sprouting in the suburbs are not following the architecturally imaginative lead of companies such as Span: they are increasingly going over to the neo-Georgian styles and detailing that estate agents find their clients want above all else. Neo-Georgian revivalism may have been a continuing feature of British commercial and institutional architecture since the beginning of the century. But now that it has largely departed from that scene, we find it creeping into the field of private housing. Could one not suggest that when the town environment becomes dominated by materials such as glass, concrete and steel, people yearn for more human surroundings when they get home?

However fanciful such an analysis of public taste may be, there is no denying its vigour and its capacity to respond to changes in its physical environment. Nor can it be denied that the direction in which it is moving shows quite clearly that people are reacting—

albeit subconsciously—against those aspects of their physical surroundings which are concerned with scale and proportion. This development, coupled with the more direct concern with urban conservation as such, I believe heralds a significant new turn in the public's attitude towards the type of city they want to see London becoming.

This is all very well. But it could be argued with reference to many of the streets I have described—and to even more that I have omitted—that the horse has already bolted from the stable. The fact that the public is gradually awakening to the importance of scale and quality in urban re-development may be gratifying in theory, but is this awakening not too late? The re-development of virtually all the central areas of London that has taken place since the war has been drastic, leaving hardly a street, square, park or vista unaffected. This fact has given added force to the arguments of those who rightly believe that cities must evolve from one age to the next, but who add that this inevitably entails the overwhelming if not the destruction of what went before. Cities, they say, must change or die. And the circumstances under which they must change today are necessarily drastic. By all means, so the argument runs, preserve the architectural 'museum pieces', but it would be suicidal for London to deny free scope for commercial re-development or not to provide fully for the use of the motor-car. The economics of modern commerce and of modern administration in city centres demand high densities that can only be achieved by building up. And the exercise of free movement round the city by people, goods and services in conditions of reasonable speed and comfort is equally vital if people are to go on living and working there.

There is obviously a basic truth in this point of view which it would be pointless to challenge. Besides, the soaring towers of the City of London and of numerous other developments in the Inner London area, as well as countless comprehensive re-development projects, are sufficient evidence of its *force majeure.* London is by no means dead and is 'evolving' economically in a manner healthy enough to ensure its survival at least into the foreseeable future. The point, however, is that its citizens are now concerning themselves with this evolution in a new and vigorous manner and have shown in a variety of ways that they do have a general concern and definite views about what course it should take. They want the right—which they have—to conserve what they feel to merit conservation, to criticise the design of new developments and to control the impact of such developments on the existing environment. They do not accept that a private developer can do precisely what he likes with land that is his. And increasingly they are coming to accept that the limitations imposed on such re-development can be concerned with considerations of visual amenity and aesthetics as well as stricter matters such as the size and the scale of a particular building, and the social effects of the various uses to which it might be put. All these principles have already been enshrined in various planning and conservation laws, but only now is pressure building up behind the application of their spirit as well as their letter. There is little doubt that scarcely a murmur would have been raised just ten years ago against the destruction of Carlton Mews or Woburn Square—both of which were greeted by a furious public outcry when they finally occurred in 1969. And it is most probable that had planning approvals come forward today for either project, they would both have been refused. Similarly, it is unlikely today that Shell would get away with a development of the ugliness of their South Bank Centre in the existing climate of opinion. However, there is still a desperate need for an advisory institution to act as a pressure group on the planning authorities that can work in a more independent context than the architect-dominated Royal Fine Arts Commission.

This greater public concern with the manner of London's development since the war is, I think, the natural and inevitable outcome of the form it has taken. For the reconstruction of London after the devastation caused by the Blitz and after the lull in normal evolution created by the war itself, has been one of the most depressing of all the chapters in the capital's history. In the light of this, it is intriguing to compare this phase of reconstruction with that which occurred after London's previous great traumatic experience—the Great Fire of 1666. For the problems faced by the authorities were remarkably similar—even if the results were naturally and dramatically different.

In the years following the last war, as in the late 1660s, there were certain imperatives with which the authorities were confronted. Absolute precedence had to be given on both occasions to getting roofs over heads and to getting businesses going again as quickly as possible. This meant that there was little leeway to seize the otherwise golden opportunities for major street engineering and the imposition of new layouts. In the twentieth century as in the seventeenth, visionary planners conceived of wondrous new cities they would create out of the ruins of the old. In 1666, men such as Wren and Evelyn dreamed of, and put on to paper, magnificent new baroque layouts for the City. Similarly, in 1944, Abercrombie and his successors projected dramatic new schemes with urban motorways and segregated precincts. In the event, as we saw in the Introduction, the City that was re-created after the Great Fire was still basically medieval in its layout. Residents and businessmen threw up buildings just as soon as they could get together the necessary money, labour and materials—and they did so, for the most part, on the sites they had occupied before.

As a result of the same pressures, the City that was rebuilt after the Blitz retained still the ancient medieval layout, apart from a few pockets of comprehensive re-development. And the bombed areas of the West End and the inner London estates remained basically Georgian in pattern, even where no Georgian buildings were still standing. There was simply no room, no time and no money for the schemes of the dreamers. Buildings went up as and when the owners could obtain the finance and the necessary planning consents. And in 1945—as in 1666—a chronic shortage of labour and materials resulted in a make-do-and-mend approach which might today be deplored as 'jerry-building', but to which, under the circumstances, there was no alternative.

Another similarity worth noting is that the authorities on both occasions, while they may have been powerless to impose a new pattern on the reconstructed city, thought nothing of imposing the most drastic controls on the design of individual buildings. In 1945, new buildings going up in central London had to conform to regulations governing height, spacing, access, light and a variety of other details; so in the seventeenth century the most rigid controls were imposed on the type of building that could take the place of the old Tudor City. Standard street widths were laid down and regulations controlled the scale of buildings, their spacing and the materials of which they should be constructed. Indeed, by the time of Queen Anne the building regulations had become so strict—particularly with reference to minimising the risk of fire—that builders found there was precious little individuality they could themselves convey by their own designs. Small wonder they ended up by putting all their artistic ingenuity into such mundane details as door-cases and angle-brackets, letting rip only when they got inside.

So much for the similarities between these two great periods of reconstruction; what of the differences? And is it merely the passage of time that suggests that the first ushered in an age of great architectural achievement, while the second produced little but an unimaginative mediocrity from which we are only now beginning—far too late—to emerge?

In the late seventeenth century, architectural fashion was going through an exciting period. New renaissance styles, introduced into the country half a century earlier by Inigo Jones, were now becoming widely accepted and developed. Architects such as Wren and Gibbs explored and experimented with them and produced public buildings in their own brand of English Baroque of a brilliance and originality that has scarcely been equalled. And even speculators such as Nicholas Barbon found in the classical, 'terraced' town house, a style whose conception was so graceful and human in scale that, from the Manhattan Brownstone to the neo-Georgian estate, it has remained in favour ever since.

It was also crucial to the nature of the post-Fire reconstruction that there should have been ample land for expansion. Despite long-standing restraints upon building in the 'suburbs', a combination of economic pressures and graft ensured that few areas remained sacrosanct from the estate developers. Land values, as a result, remained comparatively low and densities never reached the levels they did—and continue to do—in more compact cities such as Paris. The new architecture could be given full rein in the fields of Holborn, St. James's, Mayfair and Bloomsbury. And the city that presented itself to visitors in the days of Queen Anne was truly one of the architectural splendours of Europe.

After the war, however, it was very different. Land in the central London area soared in value, aided by the explosion of metropolitan office development. A four-storey Victorian office block destroyed by bombing was naturally replaced, if possible, by one double or treble that capacity, although the height of building remained initially under control. But worse by far was that alongside this desperate need for space was an almost complete lack of interest in questions of design. An architectural profession that had inevitably been pushed around in the war, afterwards found that the private work was simply not there. The vast majority of architects either went to work directly for government departments, or received most of their commissions from government sources. As Duncan Sandys (of all people) said when Minister of Works in 1945: 'We desire as much as anyone to maintain the diversity of design and scope for the individual talents of the architects. But first things must come first. The houses must go up and nothing must stand in their way.' The professional environment was one of a need, above all, for fast, cheap and preferably standardised construction. And the context of an austerity minded public service, however much it broadened its scope as the fifties progressed, was not one in which the younger post-war architects were likely to find the stimulus to break new ground.

But if the public sector acted initially as an enervating factor on architectural innovation, the private sector did even worse: for it is here that the major responsibility for the new character of the Inner London streets inevitably lay. Whereas in the seventeenth century the rebuilders of the City of London came to their task with the inspiration of a considerable and exciting new tradition waiting for physical expression, the rebuilders of the 1940s and 1950s had no such tradition—or at least none which they cared to recognise. The mainstream of British architecture in the 1930s was dominated by an old guard who, although they leaned heavily on the traditional classical styles and motifs, seemed at the same time to have little respect for the character of the city they were doing so much to transform. Examples of genuinely 'modern' architecture from the inter-war period in central London are confined to a few shops and blocks of offices and flats, mostly taking the Bauhaus school as a point of departure. The earlier promise of architects such as Voysey and Macintosh never materialised. And after the war was over it was the descendants of such Establishment figures as Sir Aston Webb and Sir Herbert Baker who found themselves once more in favour. As Professor Anthony Jackson has pointed out: 'With the length of the war and of architectural education, and the difficulties of setting up in independent practice, nearly three-quarters of all principal architects were [in 1950] over forty years of age and most of these had been trained in offices involved in everyday practicalities and not in the more aesthetically conscious schools. Their level of attainment was generally outmoded and mediocre producing nondescript arrangement faced in masonry carrying neo-Georgian stylistic overtones.' And he adds for good measure: 'Private practitioners of modern architecture were little more incisive . . . although visually and technically more up to date, most of [their] buildings are neither necessarily more satisfying nor more practicable or economic than their conservative counterparts.'

Thus we see that in the decade immediately following the last war, there were few opportunities to pursue the grand designs of the town-planning visionaries. But neither was there the money, the men, the stimulus or the existence of a creditable vernacular to build what had to be built in a manner that would be a valuable or even respectful contribution to the London street scene. Few buildings better typify this period than the Bank of England annexe by Victor Heal immediately to the east of St. Paul's in the City. It is a long, boring red-brick building in a neo-Georgian style, which winds its way round the eastern side of St. Paul's Churchyard, dominating and debilitating a huge area. It is lifeless, styleless and horribly permanent. And even where this generation did make a few nods in the direction of modernity—as at English Electric House on the Aldwych corner of the Strand, or in countless blocks in Oxford Street and High Holborn—aesthetics always seem to have been forgotten in a welter of plot ratios and reinforced concrete.

As Oliver Marriott has said in his discussion of the property boom of the fifties and early sixties: 'What the developers wanted from their architects was a commercial service. They needed functional buildings designed to a certain price, usually the lowest possible, that the estimate should not be exceeded at the end of the day, and that the architect should organise the builders such that the development was finished on the specified date.' And he adds: 'This should not necessarily have precluded the architects from designing attractive buildings, though it certainly strained good design, and the blame has probably been weighted too heavily against the developers. They were just not concerned with design. But the architects could surely have produced fine buildings within their corset of cost.'

The heart and soul of areas such as the alleys north of Fleet

Street, which had been bruised but not destroyed by bombing, were ruthlessly ripped out, simply because no one had the determination to protect them or the imagination to produce stylish or sensitive infilling of the bombed sites. The back streets of Holborn were once some of the most vital and attractive in central London and even before the last war they still contained corners of immense character: character that could well have been retained, even with much great densities, had the will existed. To wander round them today is one of the saddest experiences in London. Their buildings are lacking in any sense of style, proportion or concern for their environment. They are, in a nutshell, what distinguishes the post-war re-development of London from the city that was re-created from the great conflagration of 1666 by the architects and developers of the seventeenth century.

However, the present state of such areas does not really concern us here—although the lessons of neglect and carelessness on the part of planners, architects and clients which they present, cannot be emphasised too often. They are mistakes of the past which, because they are enshrined in buildings, will live on until they are demolished; but to the conservationist they must be considered a lost cause. They did, however, contain one negative virtue for which, from more recent experience, London should consider itself lucky. For the most part, they were not high, and did not impose their mediocrity on streets and areas that still possessed a distinctive character. To that extent they remained firmly within a tradition of urban re-development which, in the course of the last decade, has taken a severe battering. This battering has resulted from the use of new materials and techniques of construction more radical in their impact on building methods than any previous innovation has ever been. And it is in their effect on the London environment that lies the major qualitative distinction between the present re-creation of London and all those that have gone before.

In a recent book on *Towns and Townscape*, the planner Thomas Sharp lays great stress on the factors that go to make up a street 'view': the balance between variety and consistency in the appearance of a group of buildings and the importance of foci such as public buildings and church spires. Although few people, when they look at a street or experience its changing appearance as they move along it, are at all conscious of why they like or dislike it, there is no doubt that they can have very strong feelings one way or the other. Just as most visitors to Whitehall or Belgrave Square will say they find them pleasing sights, similarly few could be found to say much complimentary about Oxford Street or Kingsway—despite the fact that the architects of buildings in both the latter streets presumably felt their work to be aesthetically satisfactory. Most people would certainly accept that there is something in the combination of overall perspective and detailed form in a street that 'comes off'—and which can be ruined by the intrusion of an obstacle to that perspective or by the use of strange materials, clashing styles or overbearing proportions in its buildings.

London, as we have seen, developed in such a way that instances can be found of successful townscape from almost every age. And equally important, it contains brilliant, if fortuitous, examples of the amalgamation of styles from different ages in one street or neighbourhood. Scraps of Bloomsbury still just manage to convey an undiluted atmosphere of Georgian London. Some streets in the City still reek of Victorian commercial self-confidence. And Whitehall still presents one of the most outstanding combinations in Europe of different styles from different ages blending together in a remarkable harmony. Re-development has always possessed the capacity to destroy such consistency, and frequently—particularly in the Edwardian period—it has done just that. But the developers used always to be operating under severe limitations in this respect. The central area sites on which they built were usually too small to have too wide an impact on surrounding streets. They lacked the techniques which might have enabled them to build wide and high—indeed for a long time it was thought that London clay would never support very high buildings on the New York scale. And the traditional materials of brick, stone and stucco used on their façades seldom clashed with one another and could often produce a pleasing textural variety. The only cases of serious visual intrusion tended to be church spires; but these, by the nature of their design, tended to rise naturally and gracefully from the line of surrounding rooftops, emphasising by their tapering shapes the solidity of the street buildings beneath. Even that great exception, St. Paul's, which must have intruded with an awesome presence over the streets of the Georgian City, still seems when viewed from Waterloo Bridge to respond to its surroundings, with the curve of its dome and the classical detailing of its towers, rather than glare down at them as do the point blocks farther west.

In the last decade and a half, all this has changed. Commercial pressure has combined with the rapid development of steel construction to secure a relaxation of high building controls. And there has been a total confusion among the planning authorities in regulating the siting of the resulting tower blocks. Countless memoranda were produced on the potential threat these developments posed to London's architectural amenity. Numerous controls have always existed, including enough 'teeth' to have put a stop in theory to virtually every tower block now standing. The consequence, however, has been almost worse than if no one had ever suggested visual intrusion was any problem at all. For the planning authorities came to believe for a time that, in contrast to American policy, a high building in London should best be treated as architecturally akin to a cathedral or church spire. It should be seen separate and on its own—as a 'point block'. Since all such blocks have been straight up-and-down jobs, usually emphasising volume and mass rather than height and seldom paying any attention whatsoever to roof-lines or to the materials or styles of surrounding buildings, such a policy was an aesthetic nonsense. But more serious, it prevented what should have been the really exciting development of high building clusters in areas where such high densities were inevitable, such as the City of London. As a result, the City itself is full of half-hearted medium-height buildings, designed to absurdly restrictive plot ratios and already looking, as along the Barbican, like paltry up-ended boxes. The City should by now be a mass of soaring skyscrapers like the Commercial Union tower or the Chamberlin, Powell and Bon flats in the Barbican. As it is, its skyline looks a mess.

Meanwhile, farther west the pass has been sold with a policy which was a flat contradiction of any concept of architectural amenity and which has done more to spoil the essential character of large areas of London than centuries of piecemeal re-development. There are today few architecturally important streets, squares or parks in inner London which are not affected by a high building at some point or other. Bloomsbury is now dominated by Centre Point at the top of Charing Cross Road, the area round Holborn is subjugated by the *Mirror* Building. Regent's Park has lost its wonderful *rus in urbe* atmosphere to the Post Office Tower and the Euston Road development—where the planning authorities ludicrously permitted some towers but not too many. St. James's has New Zealand House and, visible down its main street, the Vickers Tower on Millbank, which dominates Whitehall as well. The whole Embankment and South Bank of the river is visually desecrated by the monstrous Shell Centre—surely one of the worst bits of post-war re-development in Europe. Georgian Mayfair has been sat upon by the Hilton Hotel, devastatingly placed on the visual axis of Curzon Street and North and South Audley Streets. Three separate towers rise over the north, north-east and east views out of Hyde Park. And south across Kensington Gardens stands the citadel of the government's own Knightsbridge Barracks—designed by the same Sir Basil Spence who was a member of the Royal Fine Arts Commission which explicitly laid down that no tall buildings should be allowed to surround central London parks. Some of these buildings are good ones and a few are even of quite outstanding quality. But almost all of them have been allowed to go up in places where they do far more damage to the London scene by their impact on other buildings than any benefit they could conceivably contribute in themselves.

THE FUTURE

All this, however, must now be treated as so much water under the bridge. Perhaps, one day, some of the mistakes of the post-war period may be vigorously rectified with the judicious use of the wrecker's crane. The task now for those concerned with the evolution of London's character is the pragmatic one of identifying the quality of what is on the ground now, and seeking, in the best conservationist tradition, to preserve what is of value and importance and influencing the nature of those changes that must take place.

The framework within which new pressures can be brought to bear on the manner of London's development is a complex one. The constraints that operate on a developer—be he an individual, an institution, a private or a public corporation—are first and foremost resource ones. He is subject to a severe financial incentive to make the fullest and most economic use of a particular site, and to build his development in as cheap a manner as possible. We have seen the results of this given full play after the last war.

He is also subject, however, to his own aesthetic sensibilities and—through the operation of prestige considerations—to the sensibilities of a wider public. And if he is a public authority, these considerations may be very powerful ones indeed. It is fascinating to examine the development of modern London architecture over the past quarter-century in terms of the relative importance attached to aesthetic quality by different types of developer. An American observer, G. E. Kidder Smith, has noted the contrast, for instance, between public and private patronage in London in the forties and fifties with some surprise: 'Where the Government, or at any rate a select agency like the London County Council, has been in charge the building level has been very high; where big business, private wealth and commerce—and above all, speculative builders—are concerned, the picture degenerates into the second-rate or worse.' He might also have drawn a contrast between the London County Council, where the quality has been highest and grass-roots political pressure strongest, with the central government departments who have had less concern for their public image and have casually thrown up blocks such as the Ministry of Defence in Whitehall and offices in Horseferry Road. The overall picture is, however, less unhappy today. As yet another indication of mounting public awareness of environmental quality, British industry and commerce do now feel the need to invest in prestige in architecturally new and exciting ways—as their New York counterparts have been doing for years.

These constraints may be important ones—though they have taken a long while to operate—but they could never be considered sufficient. Nor, since the earliest town-planning legislation, have they been regarded as such. Other constraints on the developer's freedom to alter the character of existing townscape are legislative, administrative and professional. The most important and the best known is the procedure for the protection of buildings of historic interest. These buildings, including in London virtually every work dating from the Georgian period or earlier, are listed by the Ministry of Housing and Local Government, and a special 'listed buildings consent' is needed to pull them down or in any way alter them. The Ministry also keeps a supplementary list of buildings considered of historic interest, but not meriting statutory protection, This list (known as Grade III) is chiefly for the benefit of local authorities in vetting planning applications; it includes a large number of Victorian and Edwardian works, and now that the Ministry has started listing buildings after 1914 it will presumably soon include some modern works as well.

The impact of 'listing' on the London street environment has obviously been immense. Despite the swift development of the central area of London in the past century, resulting in most of the main thoroughfares degenerating into streets of little real character, superb pockets of architectural resistance still stand out, turning areas which might otherwise have become totally barren from a visual point of view into a fascinating, if slightly inconvenient, architectural museum. Where, for instance, would Holborn be without Staple Inn, Lincoln's Inn Fields without its Palladian Nos. 57–60, or even Westminster without Smith Square and Lord North Street? The chief task now is to widen the range of the listing of London buildings to include many more which should receive protection but which, often for reasons of fashion or simply because inspectors have not got round to reassessing them, are at present at the mercy of developers. Many of these buildings are indeed on the Ministry's supplementary list, but are fast disappearing before their true quality has been fully recognised. One tremendous boost to the preservation of London's architectural heritage in this respect would be for all Grade III listed buildings to be upgraded to Grade II. This could be done, quite simply, by the stroke of a Ministerial pen. It would not ensure the protection of all buildings that could, even remotely, be considered of historic interest—many of these are still outside the lists altogether and the Ministry can always, of course, grant listed buildings consent to alter or demolish. But it would at least ensure that public opinion could be roused and the merits of a particular work debated before the demolition men moved in. It is the apparent suddenness with which the destruction of buildings such as Woburn Square was thrust before the public in 1969 that was one of the least pleasant aspects of that sorry affair. Nor was this the fault of the developers, London University, who adhered strictly to the letter of the existing procedures. It was simply that the procedures were inadequate.

However, the legislative protection of buildings of intrinsic architectural and historic interest is only a small part of the conservation of London's townscape. In this respect, the 'preservationist's' task is a comparatively easy one—given sufficient sanctions and an adequate inspectoral and policing system (which the recent clandestine alterations to the Guildhall proves we do not yet have). More problematic by far is what might be termed constructive conservation: maintaining the visual character and identity of a street or neighbourhood, or even seeking to enhance it, actually in the course of its evolution and re-development. This is something which depends not on the simple preservation of particular buildings but on the whole mix of varying perspectives, of styles, materials, rooflines, high and low buildings, and even street furniture that go to make up a street's appearance. It involves the preservation of particular buildings not for their historic or even aesthetic interest but because they contribute to a harmonious—and possibly an exciting—whole. And, above all, it involves looking at new buildings not just in themselves but in their relationship to other buildings round them. It involves what in architectural circles is known, and far too often forgotten, as the art of infilling.

Although such principles clearly have application in every corner of central London, they must be considered something of a lost cause in the inner 'museum' area: the City of London, south Holborn and Westminster east of Trafalgar Square. The most that can be hoped for here is that those 'cases' that survive—such as the Inns of Court—will not suffer from the visual intrusion of high buildings. But it is in the area immediately beyond this inner core, the area of the eighteenth- and nineteenth-century estates, that the great conservationist battles of the 1970s will have to be fought. North and west of Trafalgar Square—in St. James's, St. Marylebone, Belgravia, Kensington, Bayswater—there is still some of the finest town architecture in Europe, and variations on its theme can be found in corners of most of London's inner 'suburbs', in Kensington, Camden Town, Islington, Southwark and Kennington. These areas were developed from the early years of the eighteenth century and as such were predominantly classical, as opposed to medieval, in conception. Their layout was planned as a visual unity. Its basis was the urban square which, although derived by Inigo Jones from Italy, was London's most positive and lasting contribution to the history of town planning. Indeed, it was more than just a square. As Sir John Summerson has written of the Earl of Southampton's development of Bloomsbury Square in the seventeenth century: 'He realised that a square was not enough by itself; it had to be the centre of a residential unit comprising a market or shopping-centre and a number of smaller, less expensive streets. In fact, the whole thing had to have a life of its own.' Equally important was that the individual terraces and ranges of buildings within the pattern were designed to achieve a stylistic consistency. This type of development was by its very nature a fragile one. It depended on overall scale and individual proportion. And since the unified terraces were often massive—some of the Nash terraces in Regent's Park are over 300 yards long—they required subtle perspectives for their scale to be appreciated.

Areas with such characteristics are the essence of London. The Georgian and early Victorian architects and planners could invest their streets and squares with precisely the qualities that modern cities still need to be made human and habitable. They are qualities which are invaluable as an escape from the glass and concrete heart of the capital; qualities that cities must possess if, over the coming decades, they are not to see a perpetual flight of population to the seclusion and human scale of the suburbs and the countryside. And they are also qualities which will, in years to come, be most sought after by visitors avid for cities that have not succumbed totally to the overbearing scale of modern urban development. Aspects of London's environment that many people today lament as uneconomic could in the none-too-distant future be one of the city's most valuable assets.

No one should deny that even these areas of London must change, although they need not change as radically as the central core has had to do. But the change should take on selective and sophisticated form. Existing historic-buildings legislation provides protection—as in the central area—for most of the finest buildings. The surviving Georgian houses in neighbourhoods such as Mayfair and St. James's are mostly protected, though many later works (such as many by the school of Norman Shaw in West London) remain seriously and scandalously vulnerable. And grand schemes such as John Nash's Regent's Park and Carlton House Terrace are assured by the good work done on them by the Crown Estates Commissioners—late, but better late than never. But the problem, as we have said, is not of specific buildings but of areas in need of comprehensive conservation. Although early post-war town-planning legislation paid lip-service to environmental considerations in the powers it gave local authorities over the vetting of planning applications, the first crucial legislative step was taken with the passage of Duncan Sandys' Civic Amenities Act in 1967. It formally set out the concept of a 'conservation area' as an area of 'special architectural or historic interest, the character or appearance of which it is desirable to enhance'. Areas were to be delineated by local planning authorities —in London, the London Boroughs—and when an application is made for planning permission in or near a conservation area, the proposal must be advertised and any consequent representations taken into account before the application is determined. Local authorities are also able to give grants and spend money on rehabilitation and maintenance of listed buildings in a conservation area.

Some impact of this new awareness of the need for a comprehensive approach can already be seen in operation: the brilliant restoration of Westbourne Terrace in Paddington is one example. But the Act cannot yet be regarded a success. The requirement on publicity is a useful small advance, but the Act gave no real new teeth to the conservationist cause. Strictly speaking, it made no difference to the controls that are in existence already and which have been found time and again to be wanting. When, as so often happens in London, the local authority is fundamentally sympathetic towards the intentions of the developer, there is little incentive for anyone to worry too much about observing the spirit as well as the letter of the Act. Nor can much assistance be expected at present from a central government that has shown itself over the past few years remarkably unsympathetic to the quality of the London environment. We have not only seen the patent decline in state patronage of good architecture typified by the post-war creations of the Ministry of Public Building and Works, but we have had a series of government developments which flatly contradict the principles of the conservation legislation which the government itself is supposed to be executing. The leering dominance of the Knightsbridge Barracks over the Park and over the Montpelier Square district and the proposed destruction of the west end of Whitehall are absolute classics of the type of re-development the Civic Amenities Act was intended to prevent. They might also form its frontispiece. Yet the Ministry of Public Building and Works is subject to no final sanction on these matters, acting as it does as a privileged agent of the Crown.

It is difficult, however, to see where tougher legislative constraints than those theoretically in existence would be of much use. The implementation of the spirit of Acts of Parliament always takes longer than the observance of their letter. And in matters such as conservation, where the scope for discretion on the part of local authorities and central government is so great, it inevitably takes time for new attitudes to sink in and translate themselves to administrative practice. Sink in, however, they must. For every harmful planning application approved for a conservation area—or for any district, for that matter—can result in a defacing of the London scene that will last for generations.

One of the undoubted problems here is the simple shortage of staff in local authority planning offices who are sufficiently acquainted with the principles of conservation and sufficiently sympathetic towards the qualities of the areas over which they have jurisdiction. Whatever the background may be to particular planning decisions, the most outrageous mistakes continue to be made—such as the siting of the Hilton Hotel on Park Lane or, to take an opposite case, the banning of a high block over Euston Station when others were being permitted close by. The inner London Boroughs still have nothing that could be graced with the name of a high buildings policy, and still allow themselves to be swayed by specious arguments from development companies—particularly on the subject of new hotels. These are, at present, the biggest menace to the Georgian areas of London, which many of their customers have presumably come to admire. With more flexible plot-ratios, new hotels do not have to be high, nor do they have to be in precisely those areas where they are doing most harm to the environment. It is still not too late for absolute blanket controls to be imposed on high rise development over the whole inner London area: zones should be clearly established where tall buildings will be permitted—indeed actively encouraged—while there should be others where none will be even contemplated. A failure to make such a stand, however, will simply continue the present desecration by slow attrition of the skyline of Georgian London that has already taken place round all the central parks and down countless West London streets.

Another field in which responsibility must be heaped fair and square on to the shoulders of the planning authorities is the handling of comprehensive re-development. Comprehensive redevelopment in London has almost invariably been the arch-enemy of conservation, imposing a degree of homogeneity on to the townscape which can never compensate for the ever-changing variety that is the character of most London streets. It is not only the laziest form of rebuilding, but it has been bolstered by the eternal desire of architects and their clients to erect monuments to themselves, aided by the sudden development of new construction techniques that can make those monuments truly massive ones. The desolation created by Sir William Holford and the City Corporation round St. Paul's, or by Watney's at Stag Place in Victoria, or by the L.C.C. at the Elephant and Castle, should be an object-lesson to the next generation of town planners and architects. That few people appear to want to shop in such soulless surroundings as these developments have produced is one of the most encouraging signs of the continuing vitality of modern Londoners. To make new developments attractive to live, work, play and shop in is not an easy task, and to do it at the high densities required on most central London sites is even less so. But it can be done—and in city-centre projects in other parts of the country it has been done. The great need is to blend the demands of conservation with those of comprehensiveness.

Opportunities still exist in central London to do this well—at Covent Garden and in the Carter Lane area to the south-west of St. Paul's. The temptation in these areas to 'pull it all down and start again' is strong and the signs from the draft plans so far produced are not encouraging. But the relaxing, human scale characteristics of both neighbourhoods must be retained if they are to be re-created, as their planners hope them to be, as places in which people will want to live and enjoy themselves rather than simply find themselves an office. Both should be test cases of imaginative and constructive conservation, for they are both among the most important sites in London.

Here, of course, much of the responsibility for conservation passes from the planner to the architect, and to his relationship with his wider public. The constraints we have been examining can only operate effectively, the authorities can only plan sensitively, if the architectural profession can carry conviction in wanting to enhance London's appearance, and if people can feel sufficiently involved in its evolution not simply to shrug their shoulders and escape to the suburbs. One of the greatest challenges to an architect working within a particular townscape should be not to see how far he can produce a monument to his own originality and genius but to produce buildings that contribute something new, exciting and sympathetic to the existing environment. The art of 'infilling' is a sadly neglected one in the architectural profession, and examples of its successful application in London are few and far between, especially when set alongside the instances of its failure. Yet the establishment of a vernacular of modern architecture that can provide the necessary improvement in space and accommodation in inner London without tearing the aesthetic guts out of neighbourhoods is absolutely essential—unless we are to end up with Portman Square repeated a hundred times over. As Roy Worskett says in his recent book on the *Character of Towns*: 'In historic towns there is a public interest beyond that of client and architect. No developer or architect has the right to destroy the quality of an ancient street or the setting of a historic building. This does not concern only the building next door and the need to design in sympathy with it. The new building must be influenced by the qualities of the whole group of building into which it must fit . . . all too many architects neglect this aspect of design.' Another way of saying this is that less publicity should be given to the Centre Points and New Zealand Houses of London (however good they may be in themselves), and more should go to such quietly imaginative exercises in infilling as the four-storey, glass-walled block in Dorset Square, Marylebone, or the Hille Showrooms in Albermarle Street, or the brilliant modern flats in the middle of Sloane Street, or even the simple Barclays Bank on the corner of Markham Square, Chelsea. These are all buildings that do something for their environment, rather than thumbing their noses at it, as Richard Seifert's Centre Point so blandly does.

People, in the last resort, must be brought to recognise that this is what an evolving city is all about. And here we come back to where we began. No system of collective controls will be effective if people are not aware of what they are intended to achieve. I outlined at the start of this chapter, the extent of the new public awareness of environmental quality that has arisen over the past few years, and I warned that there was a danger of reaction setting in against the ideas of modern planners and architects about the type of city they apparently wanted to create. At present I believe the concern to be there, but not yet the sophistication. A city that will rise up in munificent anguish at the prospect of losing such great works of art as a Leonardo cartoon or a Duccio, can still show an appalling apathy towards the disappearance of the uniquely English art that is enshrined in so many London buildings. And while we pummel our schoolchildren with endless instruction in the history of painting and sculpture—arts which many of them find alien and to which most of them will never return—we tell them virtually nothing of the art of architecture which they are seeing all about them every hour of the day. It is in failures such as this that the real danger to the future identity of London lies.

That danger, however, is still a long way off. London's character can still be appreciated by those who care to make themselves aware of it, and can still be enhanced by the planners and architects who are working on its re-development. London remains, of all the world's great capital cities, the most supremely *habitable*. And that, after all, is what cities should be about.

Index

(For streets see Contents)